D1242296

HBR Guide to
Negotiating

Harvard Business Review Guides

Arm yourself with the advice you need to succeed on the job, from the most trusted brand in business. Packed with how-to essentials from leading experts, the HBR Guides provide smart answers to your most pressing work challenges.

The titles include:

HBR Guide to Better Business Writing

HBR Guide to Building Your Business Case

HBR Guide to Coaching Employees

HBR Guide to Finance Basics for Managers

HBR Guide to Getting the Mentoring You Need

HBR Guide to Getting the Right Job

HBR Guide to Getting the Right Work Done

HBR Guide to Giving Effective Feedback

HBR Guide to Leading Teams

HBR Guide to Making Every Meeting Matter

HBR Guide to Managing Stress at Work

HBR Guide to Managing Up and Across

HBR Guide to Negotiating

HBR Guide to Networking

HBR Guide to Office Politics

HBR Guide to Persuasive Presentations

HBR Guide to Project Management

HBR Guide to
Negotiating

Jeff Weiss

HARVARD BUSINESS REVIEW PRESS

Boston, Massachusetts

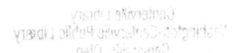

HBR Press Quantity Sales Discounts

Harvard Business Review Press titles are available at significant quantity discounts when purchased in bulk for client gifts, sales promotions, and premiums. Special editions, including books with corporate logos, customized covers, and letters from the company or CEO printed in the front matter, as well as excerpts of existing books, can also be created in large quantities for special needs.

For details and discount information for both print and ebook formats, contact booksales@harvardbusiness.org, tel. 800-988-0886, or www.hbr.org/bulksales.

The web addresses referenced in this book were live and correct at the time of the book's publication but may be subject to change.

Cataloging-in-Publication data is forthcoming.

ISBN: 9781633690769
eISBN: 9781633690776

The paper used in this publication meets the requirements of the American National Standard for Permanence of Paper for Publications and Documents in Libraries and Archives Z39.48-1992.

MIX
Paper from
responsible sources
FSC® C101537

What You'll Learn

For many people, negotiating may be scary or unpleasant. You worry that you may not have the right skills to go head-to-head with someone and get what you deserve, or that you'll damage your relationship with your boss, customer, or colleague in the process. You fear that the negotiation will escalate into hard bargaining or a heated debate and that, in the end, one of you is going to have to give up something you want just to reach an agreement.

But negotiations don't need to be stressful. You can work with your counterpart to get what both of you want in a more productive, positive way. In this guide, you'll learn a collaborative and creative approach that results in better outcomes and stronger relationships. It works in any situation in which you and a counterpart need to come to terms despite competing interests—from formal multimillion-dollar sales agreements to informal conversations with colleagues about how you will tackle a quick project.

You'll get better at:

- Identifying the real issues at stake

- Overcoming your assumptions about the other party

- Preparing materials in advance

- Setting the right tone as you begin the conversation

- Coming up with potential solutions that work for both parties

- Narrowing down your options

- Handling emotions in the negotiating room

- Recovering when communications break down

- Taming the hard bargainer

- Knowing when to walk away—and how to strengthen your fallback plan beforehand

- Managing multiple-party negotiations

- Reality-proofing your agreement

- Learning from your negotiation

Contents

Contents

Section 4: POSTGAME
Careful review drives learning and improvement

Introduction

Negotiation is about creativity, not compromise.

Whether you're aware of it or not, you're negotiating all the time. When you ask your boss for more resources, agree with a vendor on a price, deliver a performance evaluation, convince a business partner to join forces with your company, or even decide with your spouse where to go on your next vacation, you're taking a potentially conflict-filled conversation and working toward a joint solution. That's what a negotiation is—a situation in which two parties with potentially competing incentives and goals come together to create a solution that satisfies everyone.

It's not just high-stakes, months-long discussions that warrant a thoughtful approach. Improving your ability to handle all of these situations pays off. This means honing skills such as conflict management (as you'd expect) and creative thinking (which you might not), both of which are critical to reaching mutually beneficial decisions.

I've heard many people say that being a good negotiator is about thinking quickly on your feet or being a better orator or debater than your counterpart. Sure, those things are helpful. But the best negotiators—the ones who most often get what they want—are those who are the most prepared and the most creative.

This guide will help you develop the skills to negotiate like them so that you'll be more effective at work—and even get that trip to Maui on the calendar.

The advice in this guide is meant for professionals at all levels. You may have years of experience under your belt or be relatively new to negotiation. It is also applicable to negotiations of any size, whether you're the lone person at the table or have a team supporting you. Throughout the guide, I'll give examples of negotiations large and small to show you how the tactics I recommend play out.

Rethink Your Approach to Negotiations

There's a popular misconception that in a negotiation, you can either "win" or preserve your relationship with your counterpart—your boss, a customer, a business partner—but you can't do both. People assume they need to choose between getting good results by being hard and bargaining at all costs or developing a good relationship by being soft and making concessions.

That way of thinking causes the typical negotiation to go something like this:

Party 1: Here's what I want.

Party 2: Here's what I want.

Party 1: OK, I'll make this small concession to get closer to what you want. But just this one time.

Party 2: OK, since you did that, I'll also make a small concession. But just this one time.

Party 1: Well, that was the best I can do.

Party 2: Me, too.

Party 1: I guess I need to get my boss involved (or find someone else with whom to negotiate).

Party 2: I may need to walk away, too.

Party 1: Maybe there's something I can do. What if I make this additional concession?

Party 2: That would help.

Party 1: I'll need to get a concession from you then.

Party 2: OK. What if we agreed to split the difference?

Party 1: It's a deal.

Sound familiar? This is a common approach, often called "positional bargaining." People believe that if they go into the negotiation looking stern and unmovable, and then make small planned concessions and not-so-thinly veiled threats along the way, they'll have more influence and get the results they want. But in my view, that isn't a path toward negotiation that gets you what you want. It's simply a haggle, a concessions game that forces you (and your counterpart) to compromise.

Positional bargaining isn't all bad. It can be quick and efficient. It requires little preparation other than knowing what your opening offer is, what concessions you're willing to make, and any threats you might use. And in the end, it always feels as if you got something, because if your counterpart played his role, then he conceded as well. In fact, positional bargaining works well when you are negotiating simple transactions that have low stakes and you don't care about your ongoing relationship with the other party (think about agreeing on a price for that leather couch off Craigslist).

But this approach can be dangerous. In almost all business negotiations—requesting a raise with your boss, resolving a conflict with a customer, convincing others of a change in policy, agreeing on a budget for next year, for example—there is a lot more at stake, and chances are strong that you'll need to continue to work with the other party going forward. If you were to try to use positional bargaining in those situations, you wouldn't get impressive results. You have to be able to stand firm *and* maintain important relationships.

Positional bargaining rewards stubbornness and deception; it often yields arbitrary outcomes; and it risks doing damage to your relationships. Most importantly, it causes you to miss the opportunity to get more value out of the negotiation than you originally expected. In other words, you won't be creative and find ways to expand the pie because you'll be so focused on exactly how to divide it up.

Perhaps most dangerously, there is an underlying assumption in this approach that you're in a zero-sum game: If you gain something, the other party has to give up something in return. In the vast majority of negotia-

TABLE I-1

A critical shift in negotiations approach

From	To
What do you want?	Why do you want it?
Will you accept, or will you give up?	What are some different possible ways we might resolve this?
How about we just split it?	By what criteria/legitimate process can we evaluate (and defend) the best answer?
Saying, "I understand"	Showing I understand
Thinking my strength comes from knowing I am right, anchoring well, and effectively using threats	Thinking my strength comes from being open to learning and persuasion, being skilled at figuring out their motives, and being extremely creative

tions I've worked on, there is always more value to be created than originally thought. The pie is rarely—probably never—fixed.

To negotiate more effectively, you need to shift your approach away from this combative and compromising approach and toward a more collaborative one. Table I-1 shows how to reframe key questions about the negotiation with this approach in mind. For example, instead of asking yourself, "What am I willing to give up?" you might think more creatively and wonder, "What are different ways we can resolve this?" This helps ensure you aren't shrinking the pie but expanding it. Throughout this guide, I'll offer advice on how to make this critical shift.

The Circle of Value Approach

This shift is the foundation of what my colleagues and I call the *circle of value approach to negotiating*. This is where two parties come together to jointly solve a problem—decide on a contract, create the parameters of a new job, or delineate the conditions of a partnership. Together they dig to fully understand each other's underlying interests, invent options that will meet everyone's core interests (including those of people not even in the room), discuss rational precedent, and use external standards to evaluate the possibilities—all while actively managing communications and building a working relationship.

At first read, this may sound like a "soft" approach to negotiation. In fact, it is just the opposite: It takes discipline and toughness to truly get creative and to apply sound decision-making criteria. Taking a joint problem-solving approach does not require, or even condone, sacrificing your own interests. It is about being clear about *why* you want what you want (and why the other party wants what she wants)—and using that information to find a high-value solution that gets you both there.

This is a method that my partners and I have developed and refined over the past three decades since its origin in our work with Roger Fisher at the Harvard Negotiation Project. We apply it—along with the frameworks, checklists, and techniques shared in this guide—with corporate clients, government leaders, and students at Harvard, Dartmouth's Tuck School of Business, and West Point. It's grounded in research, but more importantly, it's based on what very successful negotiators do from the battlefields of Afghanistan to the boardrooms of Silicon Valley, from Tokyo to Johannesburg to Berlin, from complex sales and purchases to alliances and acquisitions.

The benefits of this approach include better solutions, improved working relationships, greater buy-in and commitment, and more successful implementation of solutions.

Of course, there are challenges as well. This approach requires more preparation, deeper skill, and real discipline. You'll likely need to set aside a significant amount of time in advance of your negotiation to think through your needs, your counterpart's needs, creative options, and more. Not every negotiation will wrap up in one sitting. Some may require multiple sessions with time in between to rethink, regroup with others, or revise your plan. It will take discipline to control your responses— to avoid reacting unthinkingly to what your counterpart might do or say, or to "change the game" when necessary—and to keep moving in the direction you desire. Even the simplest negotiations require thought before, during, and after as you enter and work within the circle of value.

You may feel uncomfortable at times as you use what may be an unconventional approach. Your counterpart might be uncomfortable as well. She might even interpret your openness to collaboration as weakness and think she can take advantage of you. But if you follow the advice here, she won't. In fact, you'll shape the negotiation and get the results you seek, and often much better ones than you ever expected.

Chapter 1
The Seven Elements Tool

Carefully define your
measure of success.

How you define success in a negotiation will influence how you prepare and, in turn, how you negotiate. Think through what you want to achieve: What would a successful agreement look like? How do you want to feel when you've left the table? You want to identify specific criteria that will help guide your preparation, and you'll also use these measures to evaluate the agreement when it's complete.

Beware: There are a lot of common measures that are limiting, and even dangerous. Some professionals think they've negotiated well when they've extracted more concessions than they gave up or when they've pushed their counterpart past his bottom line. Others believe that success means they avoided confrontation or an uncomfortable situation. Still others are happy if they simply reached any agreement at all.

These measures focus on the wrong things, and they can undermine your effectiveness. Using them may limit your approach, hinder creativity, and most importantly, lead you to leave value on the table because you haven't considered a better solution. It's tempting to use these measures, especially when you sense your counterpart or your boss is doing the same, but don't. Instead, use a more robust definition of success, one that meets seven criteria.

Define Success with Seven Elements

Aim for an agreement that:

- Satisfies everyone's core **interests** (yours and theirs)

- Is the best of many **options**

- Meets legitimate, fair **standards**

- Is better than your **alternatives**

- Is comprised of clear, realistic **commitments**

- Is the result of effective **communication**

- Helps build the kind of **relationship** you want

We call these bolded terms the *seven elements*. Not only do they form a helpful checklist for determining whether your negotiation was successful, they can also guide the entire circle of value approach. We'll use them throughout the book, but for now, let's focus on how they define a successful negotiation.

Satisfies everyone's core interests

By *interests*, we do not mean the preconceived demands or positions that you or the other party may have, but rather the underlying needs, aims, fears, and concerns that shape what you want.

For example, when negotiating a job offer, you may say to yourself that you want no less than $75K and a 15% bonus. But those are demands, rather than statements that explain *why* you want what you want. Do you want that money to pay off short-term debt, cover increased living expenses, travel, create long-term security, or something else? These are your motivating interests. They're important to identify because you may be able to satisfy them in many other ways, some of which might be even more valuable to you than $75K plus 15%.

Aim for an outcome that satisfies your full range of interests *and* your counterpart's; this will go a long way toward ensuring that your agreement sticks.

Is the best of many options

Options are the solutions you generate that could meet your and your counterpart's interests. During the course of a productive negotiation, the two of you will develop many options to discuss.

Your final agreement should be the best of those many options. A good negotiator leaves the discussion thinking that she and her counterpart created real value; if the outcome feels like it was the only solution possible, it's probably not a good one.

Meets legitimate, fair standards

Standards are external, objective measures that can be applied to an agreement to assess its fairness. These might be formal guidelines, such as market prices or rules and regulations; they could be common practices or precedents in your industry; or they might be a third party's informal assessment. Those evaluating the agreement—you and your counterpart, your boss, leaders at the other company, outside regulators—are going to want to know it is fair and will want to compare it against objective criteria or external principles. You can't simply have ceded to a lower price because your counterpart begged and pleaded, or won a key concession because you outnegotiated him.

In research we conducted with close to 1,000 negotiators all over the world, we found that what the vast majority of people wanted most from a negotiation was to leave feeling that they were fairly treated and that they could defend the outcome to stakeholders and critics. Most reported this as more important than thinking they got a "great deal." Aim for an agreement that would be considered fair by those in the room and outside of it.

Is better than your alternatives

An *alternative* is something you would do to fulfill your interests if you couldn't reach an agreement with your counterpart, something that would not require the other party's consent.

Typically when thinking ahead to situations in which they are unable to come to an agreement, most people simply say, "I'm not willing to go below $120K" or "My boss told us to abandon the discussion if we can't get these terms." Unfortunately, while this "bottom line" might be your desired threshold, it's often arbitrary. Instead, consider what your alternatives truly are: What would you do if you were unable to reach an agreement with your counterpart? Would you find another vendor? Could your company make the part? Or would you stop manufacturing the product altogether? And what would all of this cost you in terms of time, quality, and money?

Once you've identified these alternatives, consider which is the best one. (This is sometimes referred to as your BATNA—your best alternative to a negotiated agreement. I'll refer to it as your *best alternative*.)

Any outcome you agree to needs to be better than what you would do if you walked away from the negotiating table. If the best option that your counterpart will consider is worth less than your best alternative, by definition you're better off resorting to that alternative.

Is comprised of clear, realistic commitments

Each party ultimately makes *commitments* to do or not do certain things, to do them in a certain way, by a certain date, and so on. These promises—to provide a service, pay a fee, deliver a product, provide resources—need to be operational, sufficiently detailed, and realistic. They also need to be made by someone with the correct authority and with the approval of necessary stakeholders.

It's not just the final agreement that is comprised of commitments: Each party will likely make promises during the process of negotiating as well (to research standards, to vet an option with people back at the home office). It's important that each of these commitments, including the final one, is made by someone with the authority to do so, on both sides of the table.

After all, structuring unrealistic agreements is a waste of time. It might feel good to think you "got them," but when the agreement unravels a week, a month, or even a year later because, for example, your supplier can't realistically produce the parts you desperately need, you will likely end up wishing you had never agreed to those terms in the first place. For an agreement to be successful, it needs to be clear that each side can hold up its end of the bargain.

Is the result of effective communication

Many negotiators make the mistake of focusing only on the substance of the negotiation (interests, options, standards, and so on). How you *communicate* about that substance, however, can make all the difference. The language you use and the way that you build understanding, jointly solve problems, and together determine the process of the negotiation with your counterpart make your negotiation more efficient, yield clear agreements that each party understands, and help you build better relationships.

Open lines of communication between parties make for an effective negotiation and will make it easier to negotiate with this party the next time as well.

Helps build the kind of relationship you want

Another critical factor in the success of your negotiation is how you manage your *relationship* with your counterpart. You may want to establish a new connection or repair a damaged one; in any case, you want to build a strong working relationship built on mutual respect, well-established trust, and a side-by-side problem-solving approach.

Using All Seven Elements

Some elements have more to do with the process, or the "how" of negotiation, and some are more relevant to the substance, or the "what." You can see all seven elements and how they are used in figure 1-1.

Some clients have asked me whether it's acceptable to simply do better than their best alternative and to call it a successful negotiation if only that element of success is reached. My response is almost always the same: Aim to

FIGURE 1-1

The seven elements of negotiation

Substance	① Interests
	② Options
	③ Standards
	④ Alternatives
Process	⑤ Commitments
	⑥ Communication
	⑦ Relationship

satisfy the requirements of *all* seven elements, both the substantive ones and the process ones. Each is important to ensuring you've gotten the most you can out of the agreement. You wouldn't cut down your checklist for assessing the safety of a product, reviewing a contract, or purchasing a key piece of equipment, so why do it here? Begin with this structured approach, and stay disciplined throughout your negotiation.

The seven elements provide a useful framework to define your measure of success, and as you'll see in the chapters to come, you can use these elements to help you prepare, determine your approach in the room, diagnose and handle difficult situations, and capture what you've learned afterward. To help you with this, use the Seven Elements Tool (figure 1-2) to document information about each of the seven elements during your prep work and the negotiation itself. Think expansively, and write down as many responses as you can for each prompt. When you learn something new before or during the negotiation, or something happens that you didn't anticipate, return to this tool and update it. This valuable worksheet will guide you throughout the entire negotiation process.

Keep in mind, you won't always use the elements in the exact same order; nor will this tool remain static throughout your negotiation. You'll likely use it iteratively, coming back to the elements over and over as you gather more information.

Now that you have a good understanding of what success looks like and the tool to get you started, it's time to prepare for the negotiation.

FIGURE 1-2

Seven Elements Tool

Related Parties	Interests
	Our interests
	The other party's interests
Core Issues	Third-party interests

(continued)

(continued)

Options	Standards
Issue #1:	Issue #1:
Issue #2:	Issue #2:
Issue #3:	Issue #3:

Alternatives	Commitments					Relationship	
						Current	Preferred
Our alternatives to a negotiated agreement with this party (highlight the best one)	Elements of a framework for agreement						
	What authority do we have?					Possible diagnoses for any gap	
Ways to improve our best alternative	What authority does our counterpart have?					Possible ways to bridge the gap	
The other party's alternatives (highlight the best one)	What level of commitment do we want?	This meeting	Next meeting	End of negotiation			
	Expressing views	☐	☐	☐			
	Generating options	☐	☐	☐			
Ways to weaken their best alternative	Joint recommendations	☐	☐	☐			
	Tentative agreement	☐	☐	☐			
	Firm, signed deal	☐	☐	☐			

(continued)

(continued)

Communication	
Meeting purpose	Questions to ask/things to listen for
Desired outputs	Information to disclose
Who should be there?	Assumptions to test
Appropriate process	How to handle conflicts?

Section 1
Before You Get in the Room

The best negotiator is the most prepared one.

Preparation is the key to any successful negotiation, but few people spend enough time on it. I've had sales leaders tell me that they prepare in accordance with how long it takes to get to their customer's office. That's fine if your meeting is in Tokyo and you live in Manhattan. But it's abysmal if you're meeting the customer in Brooklyn.

Prepare as far in advance of the negotiation as possible. Take time to:

- Question your assumptions about the negotiation

- Think through what you want from the negotiation and why—and what the other party wants and why

- Get creative about your options

- Consider objective standards to apply to your options

- Assess your best alternative (and theirs)

- Plan how you'll manage communication and your relationship with your counterpart

- Lay the groundwork for a successful negotiation by reaching out to the other party in advance

Doing all of this ahead of time gives you the advantage in the room. You'll be able to better control the process and shape the outcome.

In the next chapter, I'll discuss how to overcome some of the more common negative assumptions that you may hold as you go into conversations with your counterpart. Then, in the rest of this section, I'll address how to prepare for both the substance and the logistics of your negotiation.

Chapter 2

Question Your Assumptions About the Negotiation

Develop new, more empowering expectations.

As you launch into the preparation process, you may already have a lot of assumptions about how your negotiation will go, many of them negative. You may suspect that there is only one option the other party will agree to (because your counterpart has never budged from his stated policy) or that the negotiation itself will be unpleasantly contentious (because that's always been your experience).

But assumptions like this can be dangerous and limiting: They hinder your creativity. For example, if you think the other party is going to cling to a specific policy, you'll be focused on combating it directly and unlikely to throw out more-inventive options that may actually get you and your counterpart something *better*. Or if you assume the other party is going to push hard, you might send signals that you're going to do the same, without even realizing it.

Take, for example, a salesperson working with a procurement manager. The salesperson might think, "Well, the procurement manager has never gone for a risk-sharing deal in the past, so let's not even bring that up this time." This assumption will cause him to hold back what might be a viable solution for both sides, and if the purchaser learns he's holding something back because he's underestimated him, he risks damaging the relationship. Perhaps most dangerously, the salesperson could be leaving value on the table by not mentioning the option he's hiding. A relatively simple shift in thinking—from "He'll never go for that" to "If I never try, I'll never know if he might go for some new, creative options"—can positively change the negotiation.

As you begin preparing, take a closer look at the assumptions you've already made and how they might be holding you back. Then challenge them, and see if you can shift them. Continue this process for the entire negotiation, checking to see what assumptions you've made and recasting them if necessary.

The salesperson in the example might, after all, offer risk sharing as an option: "I know you haven't been interested in the past, but we've changed how we structure these deals to address the accounting issues you raised. It might solve the pricing issue, so I wanted to test this out again and see if we might be able to make it appealing for both of us."

Even if the purchaser says no, the salesperson has demonstrated his understanding of his counterpart's interests and his willingness to be collaborative and open to creative solutions.

Be Aware of the Assumptions You Often Make

In order to go into a negotiation with an open mind, you must first become cognizant that you hold particular assumptions that may be limiting your perspective. That's not as easy as it sounds, because these notions are often deeply embedded; they often feel like objective truths rather than subjective beliefs.

Common negative assumptions fall into two categories: premature judgments about your counterpart, and those about the negotiation more generally:

About the other party

- As in the example with the salesperson, you may expect your counterpart to do certain things based on prior experience with her: "She'll never go for an equal partnership" or "She always acts nice until the very end."

- Even if you've never negotiated with the person, you guess how she's going to behave based on where she's from or her role: "People from the Northeast are aggressive; those from the West Coast are laid back" or "People in procurement care only about the bottom-line price; engineers care only about the quality of the product and are pushovers when it comes to actual cost."

About how the negotiation will go

- You may assume that business negotiations are always formal, protracted, and overly focused on terms and conditions, or that certain kinds of personal negotiations are always contentious or zero sum, such as those about asking for a raise, purchasing a car, or buying a house.

As you're preparing for your negotiation, think back to past negotiations, or other types of work situations, and list assumptions you made that turned out to be false. Try to spot patterns and identify the kinds of assumptions you typically make.

Then review the list and ask yourself which of these are pertinent to the current situation. As you do, add any other assumptions that come to mind about the negotiation at hand.

Shift Your Assumptions

Once you have a list of your assumptions, for each item, ask yourself whether it's possible that the assumption is not true and then what it would take to disprove it. Depending on how you answer, there are a number of ways to change your thinking.

Shifting your assumptions about the other party

Hard data is one of the best ways to refute a myth. Find people who know the person or organization with whom you're going to negotiate. Talk to others who have worked with him. You might even find people who have a similar job as your counterpart and can give you a sense of what the person might care about, what pressures he may be under, or what his interests might be. Gather as many facts as you can that might disprove, or at least challenge, what you're given to believe.

If you don't have access to those facts, invite some of your trusted colleagues to a meeting where you can explain what your assumptions are and ask that *they* systematically challenge them. Give them permission to poke holes in your theories, and they can help you see things from a different perspective.

Shifting your assumptions about how the negotiation will go

To address your negative ideas about how the negotiation will go, reframe them into "enabling" assumptions—ones that support a more positive outcome. (If you aren't able to disprove myths about the other party, this approach can work for her as well.)

To do so, imagine how you would act if your belief *weren't* true. This is what the salesperson did in the example earlier: Realizing his possibly faulty and debilitating assumption—that his counterpart was likely to be "yet another unimaginative procurement manager" who would never even consider discussing a risk-sharing deal, and therefore that it wasn't worth even raising the idea—he jotted down a few ways in which risk sharing *could* work (both for him and his counterpart). Armed with this list, he is ready to share this information with the procurement manager in the negotiation itself in order to both test his openness to the idea and persuade him how it could benefit each of them.

In table 2-1, I've listed some other limiting assumptions and their more enabling partners.

TABLE 2-1

Shifting your assumptions about the negotiation

Limiting	Enabling
Our interests are opposed, so we can't both get what we want.	While some interests conflict, others are shared or just different.
These negotiations are always contentious. There's no other way to handle this except to haggle and eventually compromise.	There are many ways to negotiate, and with a little discipline, I can lead the way to a more collaborative negotiation.
The other party makes poor decisions.	The other party, like all people, will do what she believes is in her best interest.
I should behave as badly as he does.	I should do what moves us in the right direction no matter how the other party behaves.
We have no choice but to go with this solution.	There are always other options, and nothing is settled unless I agree.
These people are impossible to deal with.	With the right tools and approach, I can understand what motivates them and craft an agreement that works.

Look to Be Surprised

Throughout your interactions with your counterpart, continue to look for data that challenges your assumptions. Consider assigning someone on your team to be a watchdog; his job is to keep an eye out for any evidence that proves your expectations wrong. Maybe you presumed that the other party was going to be unbending, but you notice a willingness to involve new people in the discussion or to share information that you never thought she'd reveal: It looks like it's time to revisit your beliefs about her.

Also question your assumptions anytime you get stuck in the negotiation. Go back to your list and see which of the thoughts you wrote down might be holding you back at this particular moment. If you could disprove or reframe any of them, would it help you move the process forward?

Finally, review your assumptions after the negotiation is over. Look over the list and determine what you've learned. Record the new lessons so that you don't make the same mistakes next time. (I'll go into more detail on learning from your negotiation in section 4.)

Keep in mind that many of your assumptions, even negative ones, will be proven correct once you're in the room. After all, you made many of them based on past experience, and that can be a good guide. Perhaps the other party *does* make poor decisions or *is* particularly stubborn. But shifting to a more positive belief anyway will get you beyond those limitations. If you assume that you or the other party cannot get creative, change the course of the negotiation, fix the relationship, or trust each other, you never will.

Chapter 3
Prepare the Substance

Understand interests, brainstorm options, research standards, and consider alternatives.

To be agile and creative in a negotiation, you need to prepare for both the substance and the process—*what* you will say and do and also *how* you say and do it. You've been introduced to the seven elements and used them to define what success looks like. Now you'll use the same elements to prepare. In this chapter, we'll focus on the first four—interests, options, standards, and alternatives—which outline the content of your conversation. The other three—commitments, communication, and relationships—are more about process, and we'll cover those in the next chapter.

One note: While I lay out the elements here in a logical order, it's important to remember that, in practice, things are much more fluid; you'll iterate between them throughout the negotiation. For example, it's helpful to brainstorm interests to lay the foundation so you can then generate options, but thinking about options may help you uncover interests you hadn't yet thought about. When you're actually in the negotiating room, you'll be returning to your prep work and updating it as well.

Reserve Time for Preparation

Negotiations—of any size—require time, commitment, and careful preparation. You should devote the same amount of time to getting ready as you think the negotiation will take—at a minimum. This is true for even seemingly straightforward discussions. If you've scheduled a two-hour conversation, spend at least two hours getting ready. And the more complex the issues at hand, the more you need to prepare, at least double or triple the length of time you'll spend at the table.

There are times, of course, when you won't be able to thoroughly prepare: You see your boss on your way into a meeting, for example, and you have to agree on a deadline for an upcoming report; a vendor shows up unexpectedly and wants to negotiate a new volume purchase; or a customer calls demanding a price cut. Discussions like these still require some quick prep work—or, in the worst case, just running through the seven elements in your head as you're walking down the hall—so you can understand how you'll view success and understand your and your counterpart's point of view.

Identify Whom to Involve in Your Preparation

While you may do most of your prep work on your own, it's helpful to get others involved, if not to actively assist you, then at least to provide useful information.

As you work on each element in your preparation, reach out to colleagues both inside and outside your organization who have been in similar negotiations, either with similar issues or with the same party. Invite them to a brainstorming session to talk about the other party's interests and alternatives, for example, or just to pick their brains for five minutes: "Carol, I'm doing a limited liability agreement with a new customer, and we're trying to agree on the terms. Here are the constraints; how have you done this in the past?"

Also think broadly about who will be affected by the results of the negotiation. It might be your peers, who have to implement the decision you come to; your spouse, who cares about how your salary negotiation turns out; and, in high-stakes cases, your company's CEO or the board. These folks don't need to be included in every preparation session, but it can be helpful to review your work on the seven elements with them before you go into the room; you don't want to find out after the fact that an option you've proposed isn't feasible or doesn't account for an important interest of theirs. Most people remember to do this with their boss but neglect to do it adequately with other stakeholders.

Even if no one else is affected by the outcome of your negotiation, it's always helpful to have someone else involved during preparation to challenge your thinking and ask tough questions. Find a trusted coworker to review your work with you and play devil's advocate.

Set the Stage for Your Preparations

To begin, think again about all of the parties involved in your negotiation—the stakeholders you just identified, as well as anyone else who is involved directly (the negotiators and those to whom they will need to defend the agreement) and indirectly (end users, senior management, legal, finance, regulators). Draw a map that shows roughly how all of these players are interconnected—who reports to whom, who influences whom. Once you've connected with your counterpart, you'll dive deeper into this list of people and how they'll influence the negotiation (see chapter 5), but for now, capture a quick snapshot of the players.

Then identify the core issues—the discrete points that the negotiation needs to resolve. For example, in a sales negotiation, you may need to agree on price, service, delivery date, and so forth. Thinking through each issue will help as you think about your interests, the other party's interests, and a wide range of different options.

Keep these two things—who the parties are and what the issues are—in mind as you prepare for the negotiation using each of the seven elements.

Interests: Identify Underlying Aims and Needs

Begin going through the elements by understanding your interests. This often takes more work than you might think. You may have broad desires like "make as much money as I can" or "get it done quickly" or "maintain control of the project." Or you may have an idea of what you want in your head—the $75K plus 15% bonus discussed in chapter 1. But you need to get beyond *what* you want to *why* you want it. Why do you want that particular salary and bonus? What are you going to do with the money? What is driving your desire to want to structure it with a bonus? What are your deep-down needs, aims, fears, and concerns in this negotiation? You want to be sure to identify not just one or two of them, but all of your relevant motivations.

Write down every interest you can think of. Then take each one in turn and ask why it's important. Continue this line of questioning by asking why *that* reason is important and then again why *that* reason is important. Keep asking *why, why, why.* By digging deeper, you'll get a better understanding of what you really want from the negotiation, so you can be more creative about finding solutions that yield better outcomes overall.

Consider the other party

Think about what the other party's interests might be. Your first guess may be just that, a guess. That's OK, but seek to back it up with evidence. Look at past negotiations with this particular person or organization. What was driving your counterpart in these situations? If you haven't participated in those discussions yourself, ask colleagues who have.

Talk to people who know your counterpart outside the context of a negotiation. What do they think he cares about most? Look at similar negotiations with other companies or people. What did those people care about that might inform your estimate of the current party's interests?

Think of these initial ideas as hypotheses that you can test as you gather more data, before and during the negotiation; after all, you want to be careful that you're not just making assumptions. And, as with your own interests, get more specific by asking yourself *why* your counterpart might care about each of these interests.

Consider other stakeholders

Think, too, about your list of the other individuals directly or indirectly involved in the negotiation. For example, consider why HR might care about the compensation package you are negotiating with your future boss; think about what concerns regulators who are monitoring your company's R&D alliance might have; or reflect on what the finance department might worry about in the sale you're negotiating with a customer.

Identify areas of conflict and common ground

Once you have each individual's interests listed, note where your interests overlap, which are different but complementary, and which conflict. Thinking in advance about what drives your behavior and theirs on similar issues will help you brainstorm options that take advantage of interests that complement one another or bridge the gap between those that conflict.

Options: Imagine Potential Solutions

When brainstorming options, your goal is to develop possible solutions that meet the interests of everyone involved in the negotiation.

Write down as many good, bad, and crazy ideas as you can; don't settle for one or two options. Aim for at least seven or eight, even in a simple negotiation, and many more in a complex one. Allow yourself to come up with solutions that seem unrealistic; often from those impossible options, you'll see a path toward a more viable one. Those solutions may not address every interest listed, but each should meet at least one interest from each stakeholder.

During this portion of your prep, you might come up with an option that you feel is perfect—it meets everyone's needs. But don't become too wedded to a single idea here or even worry about prioritizing your ideas yet. You want to develop as many as you can so that you can go into the room fully armed with a range of solutions. That way you'll have a backup if your perfect idea doesn't actually end up working, and you will have your eyes and ears open if your counterpart shares something new about her interests or tosses out an even better plan.

At this point, don't worry about whether you'll divulge these options to the other party when you get into the room; just be creative. If you run out of steam, go back and look at your lists of interests, pick conflicting ones from each party's list, and ask, "What can I do about these?"

Focusing on those deeper underlying interests you identified earlier is the key to this exercise. For example, when imagining the options for your raise negotiation with your boss, avoid thinking, "I want $75K and she just doesn't want to increase my salary." (There don't seem to be many options that would meet both of those broad statements of interest.) Instead, consider that you want this raise primarily to pay for the online classes you're taking at night and the increased child-care costs involved. She may be worried about keeping salary levels consistent and having cash on hand to fund the new hire she keeps talking about, too. Once you're thinking this way, you can see that one option might be to have the company pay for your courses, especially if they make you a more valuable employee—even more so if your newly earned skills would mean your boss wouldn't have to make the new hire at all.

Make smarter trade-offs

Some options you create may be simple trades: For example, you may consider that you will accept a vendor's increase in price if he provides a higher level of service.

However, push yourself as much as you can to be more sophisticated. Invent high-gain and low-cost trade-off options. Think about what kind of options would be valuable to the other party, but don't take much away from you, and vice versa.

For example, imagine you're negotiating with a customer who is buying a new piece of equipment worth several million dollars. You know that he's deeply concerned about ensuring that the new equipment will work with his company's existing equipment. If you have plenty of engineers available at that time, you might offer to have your engineers do a pre-inspection to certify compatibility, free of charge. This doesn't cost you much (since the engineers' other projects aren't taking all their time), and it meets the customer's interest—confidence in his company's ability to use the expensive new equipment.

Get some help

If you think you've come up with all the options you can, share the interests you've identified with a colleague who *isn't* familiar with the negotiation. Ask her: "What have I missed?" "What could you imagine working here?" "Is there something else I should consider putting on the table?" She may provide you with a different perspective that can lead to more creative options.

Review your list

When you think you're done, review your list of options against the interests you identified earlier and consider whether there are ways to improve them; can you revise or add to what you have so that the options better satisfy your and your counterpart's goals?

Standards: Find Objective Criteria to Assess Fairness

Next, think about what standards might apply to the situation. Standards help you ascertain what would be considered fair if someone outside was looking in on your negotiation. They can be formal, written guidelines; common practices or precedents; or a third party's informal assessment.

Consider what objective criteria you and your counterpart might apply to determine acceptable prices, volumes, payment conditions, quality standards, cancellation terms, or other stipulations of your agreement. What standard might help you select one of your options over another?

Research written standards that might legitimize your eventual agreement. You might simply search the web, or you may need to purchase industry reports, attend conferences, or perform other forms of market research. It may take a little sleuthing, but more often than not you'll find something that will help.

For example, in a sales meeting, you might use publicly available information about what other companies have paid for similar products and services. In an alliance negotiation in which you are deciding who has rights to newly developed intellectual property, you might look at other situations in your industry where each partner is making similar investments and taking similar risks. For a conversation about your salary, look for data on what other people make who have the same level of experience and work in the same industry and region as you. If you can find that data from a reliable source, both you and your manager will likely see this as a helpful standard.

If you're unable to find existing criteria, set up a process to assess fairness, such as asking a disinterested third party to look at the agreement. For example, if you're negotiating the price for a portion of your business, approach an investment banker whom you and the buyer both trust to review the deal.

Alternatives: Consider Fallback Solutions

Now it's time to think about your alternatives, or what you would do if you're unable to reach an agreement with your counterpart. Go back to your list of interests and ask yourself what you might do to meet them if you cannot come to an agreement. Jot down all the possibilities that come to mind.

For example, if you and a supplier aren't able to settle on terms, you could go to another supplier. You could stay with this supplier, but escalate the negotiation to his boss. Or you could hold out a few months and see if the deal gets better with time. In a raise negotiation, if you aren't able to agree on an arrangement that meets your range of interests, you could look for a different job, go freelance, or—in the previous example—decide not to take those classes after all.

Consider alternatives that you or your organization might simply pursue on your own (manufacturing a part yourself) as well as those that involve other parties (finding another supplier). In either case, research each alternative you identify: Get bids and understand costs and benefits so that you can understand how each alternative reflects your interests.

Strengthen your best alternative

Once you've created a list of five or more alternatives, ask yourself which best meets your interests. This is your *best alternative* and sets the bar for any agreement: Never agree to an option that is worth less to you than your best alternative.

Now ask yourself what you can do to make this alternative more valuable to you. As a simple example, if you're a manager negotiating a revised agreement with a longtime vendor, you might decide that your best alternative would be to switch to a different supplier. You've done research and identified potential alternatives and even solicited bids. But if you've identified this as your best alternative, find a way to improve those bids. You might negotiate the price with one supplier or send some of your engineers to work with her to improve her product. Doing this work up front improves your ability to resort to your best alternative: You're poised to take that option if necessary.

Weaken the other party's alternatives

Also think about what the other party's alternatives might be. You won't know for sure, but come up with some hypotheses. Perhaps you've heard he's working with another supplier, or you assume that he has another job candidate in the interview process.

Assess how you can weaken the other party's best alternative. Can you change your counterpart's perception of how strong that alternative is? Can you show him that it wouldn't be easy to change to a new supplier by demonstrating the switching costs? Or can you show that you are more valuable than the other job candidates because you're likely the only one who knows the organization as well as you do?

Here's another example: If you're getting ready to discuss an agreement with a colleague from another department and you assume his best alternative is to go to your boss instead, you might go to your manager preemptively and explain the situation: "I just want to give you a heads-up that you might get a phone call. When you do, do what you think is best, but I'd prefer you refer him back to me." If your boss agrees, then in that one easy move, you've eliminated your counterpart's ability to get a better deal by escalating the issue.

Push as Far as You Can

As you prepare each of these four elements, push yourself: Don't settle for two or three interests; find seven or eight. Come up with a whole range of relevant standards. Develop options that might seem crazy at first. Ask yourself hard questions, and if you're unable to, bring someone in to help. The harder you push and the deeper you go in your preparation, the more power you'll have at the table.

You may not be able to answer all of these questions during your preparation. If you've never interacted with the other party before, you may not know her specific interests or have a way to find out. You may not be able to uncover relevant standards. That's OK. Identifying these holes as you prepare is just as important as completing what you know. These gaps help you decide where to start when you walk in the room: You'll want to open the first meeting by asking about the other party's interests, for example, or probing about her best alternative.

Don't skip out on portions of your preparation, even if you think, for example, that it's highly unlikely that you'll need to resort to your alternative. Even if you don't end up using it, your preparation will help you make the right decisions in the negotiation. Prepare every element using the questions in the box "Questions to Answer While Preparing for the Substance of Your Negotiation" at the end of this chapter so that you are ready for anything that comes your way.

Preparing When You're Short on Time

Even if you find yourself with limited time to prepare—you're facing an immediate discussion or a customer calls you for a spur-of-the-moment chat—it's important to consider each element carefully before your negotiation. You'll need to understand the full range of solutions available to you in order to best meet your interests, even if that means looking elsewhere. In a case such as this, run through each of the elements in your mind and list all that time will allow.

For example, Annie is walking down the hall and spots a colleague, Raj, whose help she needs in staffing a new strategic project. Raj has 15 people on his team and lots of projects to which they are assigned, and Annie has the same. Unfortunately, Annie cannot get one of her priority projects done on time without the expertise of two of Raj's team members.

Annie waves to Raj, asking if she can set up a time with him later in the week to talk about the possibility of borrowing some of his people for the project. He tells her he'll be out of the office, but if she can wait five minutes, he'll be happy to discuss it today. He ducks into a conference room and says he'll be right out.

Annie didn't expect to have the discussion immediately, but she takes what time she has to prepare. She asks herself the following:

What are my interests?

- To get the new strategic project done well and on time

- To ensure my team's other projects remain on track

- To stay within a small hiring budget

- To keep up the morale of my team

- To solve the staffing problem quickly

What might Raj's interests be?

- To ensure his team's projects are not derailed

- To keep control over his resources, so he can plan ahead and have the flexibility to adjust his people's projects

- To finish some lingering projects on which his team is behind

- To avoid setting a precedent of loaning out his people, particularly during busy times

What are some creative joint options?

- Raj loans me the two experts I need for three weeks, and I loan him three people afterward to help finish up the projects on which he is behind.

- His experts agree to provide training and supervision for some of my team members and help him and his people look like heroes to the executive team.

- He and I pool our limited hiring budgets and jointly hire another person who has the expertise we both need.

- He loans me the experts, but he can pull them back any time for his own projects with two days' notice.

- We jointly make the case to our managers to extend the schedule on one or more of Raj's projects, so we can tackle my new one together.

What are some persuasive standards to apply?

- Previous instances of resource sharing when working together in the past

- How other departments or functions within our company determine resource sharing

- What we believe our managers consider are the most important projects to get done in the near term, given strategic importance, revenue-generating opportunities, and the cost of delay

- How much of the expertise I think I need tends to be required on similar projects in our industry

What are my alternatives if we can't reach an agreement?

- Negotiate with a different colleague who may have the same kinds of expert resources on her team

- Escalate the issue to my boss for help in securing the expertise needed or for additional funds to hire from the outside

- Hire someone part-time who can train my team

- Negotiate to delay the start of this project until experts are free

What are Raj's alternatives if we can't reach an agreement?

- Simply say no and focus on his own projects

- Delay the decision by saying, "I'll get back to you in a few days"

- Negotiate with others for resources that will help him get his projects back on track

- Bury his experts in his more strategic projects, so I can't make the case to management to lend those people to me

By quickly asking herself these questions and coming up with even just a few answers for each, Annie is better equipped to have a successful negotiation and knows what alternatives she can leverage if she and Raj have trouble reaching an agreement, even though time is short.

Now that you've gone through the first four elements of success, let's move on to the next three: commitments, communication, and relationship.

QUESTIONS TO ANSWER WHILE PREPARING FOR THE SUBSTANCE OF YOUR NEGOTIATION

Interests:

- What are your interests and *why*?

- What might the other party's interests be and *why*?

- Are there any third parties whose interests should be considered?

- Which interests are shared, which are just different, and which conflict?

Options:

- List a range of options that might meet different combinations of both parties' interests.

- How can you build upon these options to even better meet your interests and theirs?

Standards:

- What external criteria might be relevant?

- What standards might a third party apply to evaluate the fairness of the agreement?

- What other objective standards might be relevant to apply here?

QUESTIONS TO ANSWER WHILE PREPARING FOR THE SUBSTANCE OF YOUR NEGOTIATION

Alternatives:

- How can you satisfy your interests without the other party?

- How might the other party satisfy their interests without you?

- How can you improve your alternatives?

- How can you weaken the other party's alternatives?

Chapter 4
Prepare the Process

Plan how you will work and communicate with the other party.

Once you have a grasp of the substance of your negotiation, it's time to think about the process. Imagine that the interests, alternatives, options, and standards you've just formulated are the "what" of your negotiation. Now, plan the "how."

Commitments: Identify Milestones and Consider Who Has Authority

Think about the smaller commitments each side will make throughout the process and determine who has authority to make each of those commitments. You'll have an agreement at the end that represents the total package you've shaped, but along the way you will also make more-discrete promises, and each of those need to be realistic. Take time now to prepare how and when those commitments will be fulfilled.

Identify milestones

Start by thinking about the negotiation from start to finish. Maybe it will be one meeting, or perhaps you'll need to get together multiple times. Roughly estimate how many sessions it will take and identify a smaller goal or set of goals for each one. Even for smaller negotiations or quick hallway discussions, you'll want to delineate your plan for each touch point.

Start with the first meeting you've envisioned. What's its purpose, and what do you want to achieve? Maybe all you want from this initial discussion is to build the relationship, showing your counterpart that you're trustworthy and committed to coming up with a joint solution. Or maybe you want to walk out with a solid understanding of his interests. Perhaps you want to lay out some options for the other party to consider or take back to his boss.

Do this for each subsequent session, too, identifying what you hope to achieve at each milestone. When do you hope to have a joint recommendation? When do you want to have a signed agreement in place?

In a simple negotiation, you might plan to make the following commitments (and ask your counterpart to do the same):

Meeting 1. Generate a range of options to mull over

Meeting 2. Create a draft agreement

Meeting 3. Reach a final agreement

In a more complex negotiation, the commitments might look like this:

Meeting 1. Agree on what the core issues are and the timeline for addressing them

Meeting 2. Come to a clear understanding of interests around each key issue

Meeting 3. Create a framework for the agreement and brainstorm options for filling the framework

Meeting 4. Decide on options to review internally

Meeting 5. Define standards to apply and use them to narrow down options to a select few for you to each review individually

Meeting 6. Agree on a joint recommendation to share with stakeholders

There are two primary reasons to map out milestones in advance. First, it helps you plan for each session adequately: Walking into a meeting to define the issues to eventually resolve requires a different kind of preparation from going into a meeting to develop a full agreement. Second, it identifies set times to go back to your stakeholders during the negotiation and get their input or approval so that you can make sure that they are available at those times.

Know who has authority to make commitments

You and your colleague may be planning to discuss what resources each of your teams can give to a new cross-functional project, but before you meet, consider whether either of you has the authority to make the final call on these allocations—and if not, who does. Similarly, think about the authority of your counterpart. From whom will she be getting approval?

If you need to get approval from others, keep that in mind as you set milestones and build in time to go back and huddle with your team. Similarly, if your counterpart has a low level of authority, you need to be prepared to give her the time and evidence she needs to get the agreement approved.

Lastly, if you don't yet have enough information about your counterpart to make this assessment, note that so you can ask about the structure of who can make what commitments once you are face-to-face with her.

Communication: Plan Messaging and Process

As you prepare to reach out to the other party to begin the negotiation, think about what and how you are communicating. You'll want to think about what messages you want to send, identify what information you need, and create an agenda to send to your counterpart.

Plan your messaging

Whether oral or written, verbal or nonverbal, the messages you convey during your interaction—and how and when you do it—can have great impact on the course of the negotiation, so it pays to be deliberate. Equally important to consider are the messages you *don't* want to send.

First, think through what you want the other party to understand and how you'll convey it. You might want to express how seriously you take the negotiation, your desire to move quickly (or slowly), your level of authority, or your wish to repair a damaged relationship.

Take this example: A sales team has been working with a prospective customer for months, and they have a solution they think will work. They need to agree on details such as price and precise configuration. The team has determined the messages they want to send in the next session:

- There's tremendous value for the customer in this solution.

- The customer should focus on the total cost of ownership for this product, not simply the price.

- The product configured as discussed is $4 million apiece, but each machine will save the customer $2.5 million in increased volume and reduction in defects.

- There are other product configurations, which could bring down the price.

- Given what the customer has said about his interest in cutting costs, increasing volume, and reducing defects, the team believes this solution best meets his needs.

Now that the team knows what they want to get across, they can think about the best way to deliver those messages. They'll decide who on the team will say what, in what order, and at what points during the next session.

Know what information you need

Equally important to knowing the messages you want to send is identifying what you want to learn from your counterpart. There are likely to be holes in your preparation—things you need to confirm about her interests, her alternatives, her authority, and so forth. You'll also want to learn about how she views you, your relationship, and any past history you have. Craft a set of questions to ask in the room to uncover critical information and test any hypotheses you made.

In the earlier example, because the sales team is trying to better understand the buyer's interests and his ability to make a commitment, they might ask questions like "We talked before about downtime for this piece of equipment. How much is that costing you every day now?" or "You said there are some folks in your organization whom you need to convince. Who are they, and what are their interests?"

The team may prepare questions to query the other party for feedback on the messages they plan to present. To keep the lines of communication open, they can ask things like "Are there other interests that this solution doesn't meet?" and "Do our calculations seem right? If not, what are we missing?"

Draft an agenda

The last piece you'll need is an agenda to share with your counterpart. Use the milestones you laid out when preparing commitments and the communication goals you have for each session, and create a draft agenda. This tentative plan will help you communicate with the other party about how you expect the negotiation will go. If you plan to develop a series of options by the end of the first meeting, for example, draft an agenda that includes exploring her interests, sharing some of yours, jointly brainstorming possible options, and narrowing down to a few ideas for further consideration. Also consider who needs to be in the session. Can you and your counterpart be the only ones in the room? Do you need someone with a particular expertise, perspective, or level of authority? Include the appropriate individuals on the attendee list in your agenda.

Relationship: Plan How You Will Work Together

Whether your relationship with your counterpart is on-going or you expect it to last for only the duration of the negotiation, it pays to invest in it. It creates the foundation for the best possible outcome of your negotiation.

Identify any gaps in the relationship

Start by assessing the relationship as it stands now. Is there one? If there is, is it based on trust? Has it ever involved creative, joint problem solving? How about risk taking? Are you able to deal with differences? Has there been damage to the relationship that needs to be repaired? You may have done some of this as you questioned your assumptions about the negotiation, but take a moment to think about with whom you'll be interacting.

Then think about the relationship you want to have. Do you want to deepen trust? Encourage an equal partnership? Do you want to express emotions more openly? Or are you happy with the way the relationship is and just want to maintain it?

Examine any gaps between how you see the current state and the ideal you've described. First, assess why the gaps exist. What caused a breakdown in trust or a lack of respect? What happened to make the relationship a transactional one? Why can't you solve problems together or take risks? Why do you feel unable to share your emotions about the state of the agreement?

Take action on the gaps

Next, ask yourself what you can do to address the situation. For example, perhaps you've identified that the lack of trust a customer has expressed stems from the time you broke a key commitment. Now that you're negotiating a contract renewal, you'll know that you need to talk early on about what happened, why, and how you can ensure it won't happen again.

Or perhaps you need to agree on a plan for sharing resources with your fellow manager in an overseas office, and any communication between the two of you—never mind negotiations over touchy subjects—is awkward. This may be because you've mostly communicated over late-night e-mails and met in person only once. For this negotiation, you might decide to meet face-to-face, or at least via video conference. Leave time before you dive into the negotiation to get to know each other, discuss the pressures you're each under, and perhaps even show a little empathy for the amount of work your counterpart has taken on after hours.

When the relationship is broken

If your relationship with your counterpart is truly damaged, you need to take further steps. Focus on fixing the relationship before you address the substance of the negotiation. Take time to understand your counterpart's story about past interactions, share your own story, and try to build understanding. If the situation calls for it, actively show your empathy or plan an apology. If the problem is big, you're unlikely to solve all of the relationship challenges in just a few conversations, but aim to get the relationship to a point where you can work together in the negotiation without strong emotions getting in the way. (We'll go into more detail on how to fix a damaged relationship in chapter 6.)

When the relationship is threatened

Alternatively, you may be negotiating with someone with whom you have a perfectly good relationship, but you don't expect to see eye to eye on the issue up for discussion and worry this might strain the relationship. For example, imagine you're the head of HR and a long-standing, valued employee requests a more flexible schedule, which your company's policy doesn't provide.

Don't plan to jump in with a hard line, sharing that the policy is the policy and it applies to everyone. Instead, define an approach that respects your existing relationship, demonstrates openness and creativity, and sets a strong precedent for future dealings.

This is where the communication and relationship elements intersect: Send the right messages to keep the relationship strong. Here are some of the messages you may want to plan to send:

- You're a valuable employee.

- We want to treat you fairly and with respect.

- We are willing to be creative.

- Here is our policy and why.

- Here is how it compares with flextime policies at other organizations (including researched standards).

You may also want to ask questions:

- "Why is flextime important to you?" and "How would you use this time?" (getting to the person's interests)

- "What are your other alternatives if we can't make this work?" (the person's alternatives)

- "Are there any other ideas you have, beyond giving you flextime, for how we together might meet your interests?" (the person's options)

Instead of angering the employee by shutting him down before you have a chance to discuss the issue, you tee up a respectful conversation in which you are firm, but listen; are open to persuasion; and aim to be creative.

With a little hard work, you will find a solution: perhaps more vacation time for reduced compensation, allowing him to work at home on Mondays and Fridays, delegating some of his work to other employees, or helping him find child-care options.

On the off chance that you two cannot come to a clever solution, at least the relationship is preserved by the way you approached the discussion.

When you don't yet have a relationship

Sometimes you're negotiating with someone with whom you've never worked. Your goal in these cases is to bring the other party to trust or respect you. Think about how you might forge a connection once you're in the room. Do you know someone in common or have a shared interest? To prepare, research the person's background, using Google or LinkedIn, to identify potential connections. Also think about situations in which you've had a strong relationship with your counterpart and what contributed to that dynamic. If you're selling a product, plan to talk about other customers who were satisfied or a specific problem you solved for a client.

As you think about what kind of relationship you want to have (or avoid) with your counterpart, you'll inevitably come up with additional things on which to prepare under communication—a message you want to send, a piece of information you need. With all of the elements, approach them iteratively and return to previous ones as needed.

Anticipate Surprises

At this point, take a step back and ask yourself: What might I be overlooking? What faulty assumptions am

I making? Am I being overly positive or confident about certain elements? Am I being overly negative or concerned about others? What have I assumed is not likely that might very well happen? Review and revise your preparation based on the answers to these questions.

Then think through any external factors that might alter the negotiation. Will a competitor show up with an equally or more attractive offer? Will your counterpart get pulled from the negotiation, leaving you to interact with someone else entirely? Will someone at the counterpart's company raise a concern about working with your company? Will your counterpart's company get acquired? Might regulations change and create new risks or dictate the need for new terms?

Plan for these risks ahead of time. Write down everything that could go wrong (or differently than expected) and what action you can take in each scenario. You can't get rid of surprises altogether, but you can minimize their impact.

Some negotiators are tempted to map out tactical steps they'll take to make the negotiation go exactly as they plan. As my mentor, Roger Fisher, used to say, "It's better to have a map of the terrain than to have planned one path through the woods." Be prepared, but be flexible. You want to drive the negotiation while also listening and learning.

Most importantly, be ready and willing to be surprised, because chances are, you will be. If you prepare well, making sure to answer all the questions in the box "Questions to Answer While Preparing the Process of

Your Negotiation," you will learn from those surprises—an unexpected interest, a creative option, a persuasive standard—and the things you learn along the way can make all the difference in your negotiation.

QUESTIONS TO ANSWER WHILE PREPARING THE PROCESS OF YOUR NEGOTIATION

Commitments:

- What do you want to accomplish in your first meeting?

- What level of commitment do you want to have by the end of the upcoming session?

- What type of commitment do you want when the issue is fully resolved?

- What kind of authority do you have to make commitments?

- What is your counterpart's level of authority?

Communication:

- What is the best agenda for the upcoming session?

- What messages do you want to send?

- What do you want to learn from the other party?

- How does the other party perceive you, and how might you change that perception?

QUESTIONS TO ANSWER WHILE PREPARING THE PROCESS OF YOUR NEGOTIATION

- What did your preparation about interests reveal that you need to test?

- What other questions do you want to make sure to ask the other party?

Relationship:

- How is the relationship now?

- What kind of working relationship do you want to build?

- What are the reasons for that gap? How can you bridge it?

- What do you want to do—or avoid—in the upcoming session to develop this kind of relationship?

Chapter 5
Connect in Advance

Agree on the process and who's involved.

The final step in preparing for your negotiation is to actually connect with your counterpart. You'll want to agree on the process, decide where and when the negotiation will take place, become familiar with the players in both parties, help your counterpart prepare, and set the right tone for the negotiation as a whole.

Agree on the Process

Before you tackle the substance, talk to your counterpart about *how* you want to negotiate. This will entail some sort of conversation in advance of the negotiation itself. Negotiating over the negotiation is important and often forgotten: People like to get down to business and skip advance discussion, but if you discover deep into the process that you disagree on what the core issues are, both sides will be frustrated.

Your preparation will help you and your counterpart begin to answer the following questions. As you go, explain that you want to work together to find a solution, that you believe there are solutions that will get you both what you want, and that you want to work together using a joint problem-solving approach.

- What issues do we need to cover?

- What process do we want to use?

- Are there any other parties we need to include? When and how?

- Do we want to establish any ground rules?

- Do we want to set a timeline?

- How will we resolve conflict?

- What will we do if the negotiation begins to break down?

- Are there any specific ways we both should prepare before we begin? What are the topics around which we should prepare?

In most situations, this prenegotiation activity involves just a few e-mail exchanges or a short conversation. Sometimes this is as simple as calling your colleague and saying that before you meet next week to talk about resource sharing, you wanted to discuss who should attend the meeting and whether there are some key issues on which you and they should prepare ahead of time. Or if you're meeting with your boss to advocate for taking on additional responsibilities, this might entail sending the draft agenda you've prepared for your next check-in and asking for feedback before you meet.

In complex alliance, sales, purchasing, or acquisition negotiations, however, this initial process should be more robust. In those cases, hold a more formal "negotiation launch" to discuss these questions in detail over the course of a series of prenegotiation meetings.

Treat these initial interactions as your chance to influence how the negotiation will go, setting a collaborative and creative tone from the get-go. In our surveys of hundreds of people over time, we've seen that well over 50% of people choose an approach based on how their counterpart negotiates. Rather than leaving your negotiation up to the other person—who may well choose a poor approach—jointly shape the process before it begins.

Choose a Time and Place

After you've established what the process will be, carefully select the time and place to meet. Issues of location and timing may seem trivial, but they're not: When and where you negotiate has a large influence on how the negotiation goes and, often, what the outcome will be.

Think about the larger context for the discussion. What will have happened before, and what will come after, both for you and your counterpart? For example, you don't want to engage in negotiations with your boss about increasing your sales team's travel budget just after he's returned from a meeting with the CFO about controlling costs. Pay attention to the broader timing as well: What's happening that day, week, or quarter for your counterpart, his company, or his stakeholders?

Think about the location, too. Will you meet at his headquarters or your office? If you're having a sensitive conversation with your boss, does it make sense to discuss it behind closed doors rather than in the hallway? If you need to build or rebuild the relationship, might the initial meetings be better off somewhere friendlier than a conference room? If there are cultural or language barriers, you may want to host a video conference, rather than have a long conference call, so that everyone can see gestures and facial expressions. If you sense that the biggest barrier to an agreement will be to convince the other party of the value of your product, consider giving your counterpart a tour of another customer's site and then beginning negotiations at a nearby hotel.

Jointly choosing the time and location with your counterpart can model the approach for the rest of your discussions. Think of it as a mini-negotiation. If you force a location or time upon him, your counterpart may try to reciprocate that forceful behavior in the actual negotiation. If you tee up the logistics as a draft plan, share your reasoning, and ask for his feedback, you set the right tone going forward.

Identify the Players

It's easy to assume that if you're meeting with John, you'll be negotiating with John, but just as you have numerous constituents who care about the negotiation, so does your counterpart. Beyond John are a number of people who influence what options he can entertain, have a say in what he can commit to, and can otherwise alter the course of the negotiation. Understand who these people are and how they influence the person with whom you're negotiating.

Create a relationship map

You created a rough map of these relationships in your preparation, but now that you are in contact with your counterpart, ask who is involved in this negotiation both directly and indirectly. Build on the map you created by adding any individuals you may have missed and including all those on your counterpart's side. Figure 5-1 provides an illustration of your counterpart's stakeholders as you follow these steps:

1. Identify all the people from your party and the other party who need to buy into any agreed-upon course of action or decision. Who are the stakeholders? Don't just focus on who has the authority to approve a decision or make it go more smoothly, but think also about who can veto or derail it (step A).

2. Estimate each individual's biases. Who is likely to be supportive, and who might be opposed to the kinds of options that you've brainstormed? Think about the consequences of a decision for each stakeholder to understand where he or she might stand.

FIGURE 5-1

Relationship map

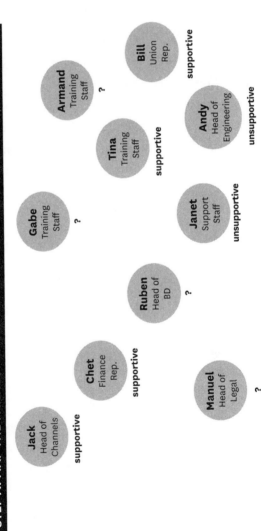

STEP A: MAP THE PARTIES AND THEIR PREDISPOSITIONS

STEP B: MAP THE RELATIONSHIP AMONG THE PARTIES

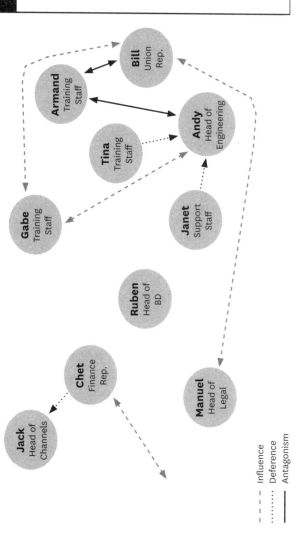

Jack — Head of Channels
Chet — Finance Rep.
Ruben — Head of BD
Manuel — Head of Legal
Janet — Support Staff
Gabe — Training Staff
Tina — Training Staff
Andy — Head of Engineering
Armand — Training Staff
Bill — Union Rep.

– – – Influence
.... Deference
——— Antagonism

STEP C: DETERMINE THE BEST SEQUENCE

1. First go to:
Jack
Chet

2. Then approach:
Armand
Bill
Ruben
Manuel

3. Next go to:
Gabe
Andy
Tina

4. Finally, approach:
Janet

3. If you are not negotiating with the decision maker herself—and you can't change the process so that you are—then you will also want to identify the "influence relationships" between the parties (step B). Is there antagonism between two people such that if Jim supports the agreement, then Heather is likely to oppose it? Who has influence over others and can sway them to support a decision? Is there anyone who defers to others and will simply support (or reject) an agreement if she knows a certain person has already accepted (or rejected) it?

You may not be able to gather all this intelligence about the other party from your counterpart. Consider other avenues for getting the information: Think back to your past experiences working with the other party, consult colleagues who have worked with them in the past, and approach mutual acquaintances who can help clarify these connections.

Use the map to influence decision makers

This map will help you get buy-in and build support, especially as you get close to an agreement. Here are three ways to put it to use:

1. **Bridge gaps in your influence.** Look for critical decision makers and influencers in the other party with whom you currently have no relationship. Create a strategy to connect with these people. Start by seeking out people who are likely to support the agreement and can help

influence pivotal but potentially unsympathetic parties.

2. **Note which relationships are antagonistic.** Determine if any of the existing relationships may be detrimental to the outcome of the nego- tiation and create strategies for managing those risks (you already did some of this in step B). Figure out how to mitigate any potential damage these negative relationships can cause. Laying the groundwork to influence a key stakeholder may take extra time, but it will also increase the odds of getting him on board.

3. **Determine a sequence for getting buy-in.** Think about the most efficient path to getting approval for the final decision, perhaps focusing your ef- forts on getting those whose support would lead others to follow suit. If you can't get the attention of a pivotal party or it will take three weeks to set up a meeting, enlist the assistance of those who have access to that person.

Help Your Counterpart Prepare

As you begin your conversations with your counterpart, help her think about how to prepare. Negotiations go more smoothly if the other party is equally equipped, and helping her along will encourage collaboration. This may seem like a radical idea (you're helping the other side!), but think about it: If your counterpart shows up not knowing what her interests are or unsure of what her best alternative may be, you may have the upper hand, but the negotiation is going to be slow and laborious while she works through what she wants.

Don't share all of your preparation with the other party, but ask questions in advance of the first meeting, either in an e-mail or in person, that prompt your counterpart to contemplate the seven elements on her own. It's much better if you both come to the table with this information in hand.

Set the Right Tone

As I've pointed out throughout this chapter, your first interactions are your opportunity to set the right tone for the negotiation. Consider the key messages you've defined in your prep work as you think about how to convey them.

You can communicate some of the softer messages about the process (for example, "I want to work collaboratively") by jointly agreeing on the time and place, asking about who else is involved, and helping your counterpart prepare. The substantive messages about the content of the negotiation require separate communications. If the messages you want to send are particularly nuanced or complex, have a face-to-face conversation.

However you choose to communicate, be deliberate so that you don't accidentally convey the wrong message. For example, if you want the other party to be put on his toes, share the fact that you have three other good job offers and that you have to decide by Monday. But if what you really want to convey is that you like the role but are interested in a better compensation package, say that.

Neither of these approaches is wrong, but you should know what tone you're setting.

Once you've agreed on the logistics and identified the relevant parties, you're ready to turn to the negotiation itself. In the next section, I'll explain how to put all of your preparation into action when you walk into the room.

Section 2
In the Room

Power comes from negotiating with discipline.

Typically, when negotiation parties have differing interests and concerns, they each start by putting a proposal on the table. Then they engage in a concessionary haggle between these opening positions. This leads to arbitrary, often lowest-common-denominator outcomes and, far too frequently, damaged relationships. Most important, it leaves value on the table.

But with the circle of value approach, negotiation needn't be a zero-sum game. We use an image of a *circle* because rather than a linear back-and-forth between you and your counterpart, you're creating a space to productively explore interests, options, and standards. With this method, you develop—and distribute—value together and work to reach an agreement that benefits both sides.

This section will help you take a more disciplined approach while you're in the discussion. You'll learn to:

1. Use communication and relationships to get into the circle of value

2. Maximize your time in the circle by exploring interests, brainstorming options, and agreeing on fair standards

3. Make a good choice by assessing your alternatives and making thoughtful commitments

In the next chapter, I'll focus on how to communicate and how to build your relationship with the other party. Then, in the following two chapters, I'll explain how and when to employ the other elements. Finally, I'll conclude this section with suggestions about how to continuously adapt your approach throughout the negotiation so that you can respond to whatever comes your way.

Chapter 6
Begin the Negotiation

Establish how you'll
work together.

Budding negotiators often wonder whether they should open the conversation at the first meeting. Should I make the first move, or should they?

Most people choose a negotiation approach based on what the other party does: They wait to see how their counterpart is going to negotiate, and then follow suit. Instead of sitting back and waiting for your counterpart to make an opening move, lead the way.

Similarly, if your counterpart takes charge, but does so in a way that you don't feel is helpful, there is no need to follow. If he opens your conversation by tossing out a position, or perhaps making a subtle threat, take a deep breath and ignore it. Explain that you'd rather work in a different way, by developing—and distributing—value together and working to reach an agreement that benefits both sides.

So what should your first move be?

Instead of laying a preferred option or demand on the table and waiting for a reaction from the other party, start by establishing *how* you will work together, invoking the elements of communication and relationship. You'll focus on these throughout the negotiation, but they're a particularly useful starting point.

Establish Effective Communication

Use this first experience in the room together to establish how you'll interact during the course of the negotiation. You laid the groundwork for this in your preparatory interactions with your counterpart, but now that you're in the room, show her how you'll work with her throughout your time together:

1. Use questions and listening skills to learn as much as possible and demonstrate understanding to the other party.

2. Make your own messages clear, confirm that you are being understood, and manage any obstacles that get in the way of your being understood.

Ask questions and listen

As your negotiation session opens, leverage what you have prepared: review the agenda, and discuss the desired goals for this meeting and what you want to have at the end of it. As you begin, ask good questions and demonstrate that you are truly listening to your counterpart.

Let's say you begin to query him about his interests. You can do this directly by saying something like, "Based on our past discussions, it sounds like what matters to you is reducing overall costs, improving quality, and decreasing downtime. Is that accurate? What am I missing?"

Then listen carefully to what he shares (and note what he doesn't). Summarize his points back to him. People want to feel heard. Check for understanding so that you have the right information and to make him feel he got his point across.

As you listen, avoid reacting to what you hear ("Oh, that couldn't possibly be that important to you" or "Wow, I want just the opposite."). Instead, absorb it and use it. You might say something like, "You really care about paying off debt and getting better training? Got it. We'll need to figure out a solution that meets those interests *and* some that I have. Are there other interests you haven't shared yet?"

Make your messages clear

Set a good example by sharing information yourself; that will go a long way to keeping the lines of communications open. Whenever you suggest an option or offer a standard, share your reasoning. But don't give speeches, either. Brevity is important. Share your ideas in consumable chunks, giving your counterpart time to absorb them and ask questions. For example, if you say too much all at once, the great point you made about needing to use a standard that your boss would find persuasive will get lost.

If you find yourself giving mini-speeches, stop yourself and ask questions instead. Test to see if you have been understood. Solicit your counterpart's reactions. See if she has some new ideas sparked by what you just shared.

Watch out for situations in which you may have misunderstood each other. If you find that you view things differently (you disagree on whether a standard is valid, for example), slow down and explore the issue together. Instead of debating who's right and who's wrong, share the reasoning behind your perspective and ask for hers. You may not see eye to eye, but reaching an understanding of why you see the issues differently will allow the negotiation to move forward.

Make sure you're engaged in a discussion, not a debate. The more your counterpart feels listened to, the more open to persuasion she'll be. If you get to a point where you can make her case as well as (or even better than) she can, you know you're headed in the right direction.

Continue to use these questioning and listening tactics throughout the negotiation.

Build the Working Relationship

Early in the negotiation is also the right time to focus on your relationship by separating it from the essence of what's being discussed in the negotiation. We call this *negotiating on two tracks*.

Negotiate on two tracks

People often believe they need to make concessions or forgo their interests for the sake of "the relationship." We've heard people say things like:

- "Well, I really like my boss, and if I act like she's not paying me well, she might feel that I disrespected her, so I'm going to just let the bonus idea drop."

- "This company is my biggest customer, and they're just asking for an extra three weeks of work, so I'm not going to risk rattling the cage by bringing up that this is out of scope and that they should pay an additional fee."

- "My customer said that he wants us to be a better partner, that we lost his trust because of how we reacted to the outage six months ago, and now he's demanding a 15% discount on the renewed contract to demonstrate that we care about him. That feels like a small concession to keep this half-billion-dollar contract."

Conceding like this in an attempt to make the other party happy is a mistake. You're not only giving away more than you should, you're also not improving the relationship itself, so you're not even getting what you think you are "paying" for. Furthermore, you're probably making matters worse: Appeasing your counterpart encourages his behavior, and you'll likely see it again and again. More important, you're not addressing the issues at stake or the circumstances that may have put the relationship on rocky footing.

To negotiate on two tracks, do the following:

- **Deal with the relationship head-on.** It may seem easier to bury relationship issues, but it isn't. If your preparation raised any concerns, or if you

75

suspect that your counterpart has some, name them, jointly diagnose them, and explore possible solutions. A strained relationship will make it difficult for you to tackle specific terms, conditions, price, and so on.

- **Separate relationship issues from the substance of the negotiation.** If your counterpart says, "If you were a good partner, you'd agree with my plan," or uses your relationship as a basis for requesting a special discount or privileged information, don't get sucked in. Instead, actively establish two tracks for the conversation. Say something like, "If you feel that I'm not being a good partner, let's discuss that. I'd like to know what you look for in a good partner, and what I'm doing or not doing, and what we both can do differently to improve our partnership. If you want to discuss the plan," or the price, or the protocols for information sharing, "that feels like something else—we should explore that on its own merits by discussing interests, options, and standards. Which of these would you like to address first?"

- **Work unconditionally to grow the relationship.** Whether or not there are existing issues in the relationship, always work on making it stronger. Set the stage for a collaborative approach from the get-go by being respectful, well prepared, and ready to listen. Always be trustworthy in your interactions. Don't worry about whether your counterpart is trustworthy or reciprocating your respect, and don't wait for him to make the first move; just do this unconditionally. Similarly, if at first your counterpart does something that you feel harms your relationship, don't take an eye-for-an-eye approach: Keep working on your end to make the relationship stronger. My former colleagues Roger Fisher and Scott Brown first talked about this in their book *Getting Together: Building Relationships as We Negotiate*, explaining that rather than reacting in kind, you should always keep your goal of a successful negotiation in mind and adopt an "unconditionally constructive" strategy for building the relationship with your counterpart.

Negotiating on two separate tracks is particularly important if you're trying to repair an already-damaged relationship; see the box "Negotiating on Two Tracks: An Example."

If you have a good relationship, but you fear that your request—a raise, additional resources, or a discount—will strain it, you can use the same approach. Raise the issue respectfully and with an openness to think and work it through together. Be explicit about the relationship factor: "I have enormous respect for you and don't want to strain our relationship in any way, and yet I have what I think is an important request. I'd love to find a way to discuss my request on its merits and in a respectful and creative manner." If you enter into the conversation and sense from your counterpart's responses that he does feel that you are hurting the

NEGOTIATING ON TWO TRACKS: AN EXAMPLE

My colleagues and I worked with an IT outsourcing company that was reaching the end of a seven-year contract with a customer. The customer wanted to sign a new agreement, but managers there were still concerned about a service outage that occurred a few years earlier. They pointed out that it had taken our client four days to respond, and the outage ended up costing them several million dollars. Trust had been broken, and the customer demanded, for the sake of the relationship, a 20% discount on what would amount to a multi-hundred-million-dollar deal.

Our client was tempted to give the discount—perhaps not the full 20% but something close—but we knew that wasn't going to solve the real problem: The customer was still not going to trust our client to respond on time, since the issues that had caused the lack of trust had not been addressed at all. Instead our client needed to break the problem in two and deal with the relationship first and the pricing for the new contract separately.

Our client then acknowledged to the customer that they had not handled the outage effectively and they understood it had led to distrust and a strain on the relationship. They also noted that while they were very open to discussing pricing for the new contract, they thought these were unrelated issues and wanted to solve them one at a time.

NEGOTIATING ON TWO TRACKS: AN EXAMPLE

Based on the ensuing discussion, our client worked with the customer to develop a new set of procedures to ensure that kind of outage would not occur again and if any other problem occurred, it would be dealt with swiftly and would involve close ongoing contact with the customer team and the CIO. They also identified the actual cost of the outage to the customer and agreed to cover this cost as part of the new deal under negotiation. They were then able to use industry standards when pricing the new contract. Thus the client was much better off than they would have been if they had unnecessarily given up millions of dollars and ignored the issues that had caused the problem to begin with.

relationship, that's the time to move the conversation to the separate track and deal with any feelings of hurt or disrespect head-on.

In all cases, your goal is to negotiate on the merits of the deal rather than making concessions or offering discounts to build rapport or trust.

Opening the lines of communication and establishing a productive working relationship allow you to move into the circle of value and then work together to negotiate a solution. You'll keep applying these approaches to communication and the relationship that you learned in this chapter throughout the negotiation.

Chapter 7
Create and Refine Your Options

Make the most of your time together.

Once you've established lines of communication and be-gun to build (or rebuild) the relationship, start discuss-ing the substance of your negotiation.

As you move further into the circle of value, you'll continue to test out your hypotheses and learn new in-formation about what the other party's interests might be. Continuously update the Seven Elements Tool you filled out earlier. Whether you do this in your head in the midst of the negotiation or update the physical document between meetings, make sure you're recording what you learn along the way.

Draw Out Interests

When preparing, you created a list of what you believed the other party's interests to be. Now is the time to clarify, confirm, deny, and add to those, as well as choose which of your own interests to convey.

This step of the process requires careful thought and discipline. Don't forget to use the tactics you learned in the last chapter about how to handle communications throughout the negotiation: asking questions of your counterpart and actively listening, as well as making your own messages clear.

Uncover their interests

To begin understanding your counterpart's interests, ask what hers might be. "What are your key aims, objectives, and concerns around the issues we are discussing?" Or, prime the pump by testing your hypotheses about her interests and fill in the gaps. Reflect back to your counterpart what, when you prepared, you suspected those interests might be and ask what you got wrong, what you got right, and, most importantly, what interests you might have missed altogether.

It's possible, even likely, that your counterpart will initially respond to these questions by stating a position: "I want a guarantee that we're getting 5% less than what your other customers pay, and I'd like you to throw in two engineers to come train my people for three months." Don't react to this. Instead, keep probing for actual interests. Ask "Why?" or "For what purpose?" or "What are you trying to achieve?" Dig deeper to find out what's driving the other party's position.

Listen carefully, because it's not often that your counterpart will come out and just say what those interests are; you'll likely have to ask a number of questions, probe deeply and even read between the lines. When you hear something that sounds like an interest, check it. "I think I heard you just say that being able to defend the price to your executive committee is important to you. Did I understand that correctly?" Adding "What am I missing?" is also helpful, because it will keep the conversation going and you might learn more.

If you're having trouble drawing out the other party's interests, suggest possible options and solicit criticism. Asking "What would be wrong with that?" can help you solicit interests from a counterpart who isn't being forthcoming otherwise: "I know this is a crazy idea and I'm not really proposing it, but what if we raised prices 20% and cut our support in half? What would be wrong with that?" It's often easier for your counterpart to point out why a potential solution won't work than to state her interests directly. (Most people will jump at an opportunity to criticize an idea. Use this to your advantage.) Then infer the embedded interests from her explanation: "I could never do that! If I did, I wouldn't be able to fund a critical R&D project; I'd have to fire people; I'd look like a terrible negotiator and might lose my own job; I'd have to personally take time to provide support to our people when I should be out developing new partnerships; or there's no way that I could justify this to my new boss."

Don't get defensive if your counterpart reacts negatively; after all, you put this forward as a "crazy idea." Instead, listen carefully: You just uncovered a gold mine of interests. Your job here is not to show that you're "right"; rather, it's to get your counterpart to tell you where you're wrong so that you can understand her interests more fully and more accurately.

Keep pushing for answers. Press for criticism. Listen for the interests within it. Test to ensure that the interests you are hearing are, in fact, her interests. Don't go so far as to frustrate her, but constructively push, listen, and test. The more interests you uncover, the easier it will be to develop creative options later.

Share your interests—carefully

It's also important that your counterpart understands the driving force behind *your* interests. Sharing your own interests may also prompt him to respond in kind. But be smart about which interests you share at this point. Though your counterpart may already know or suspect some of them, there are others that he doesn't that he could use against you.

For example, a sales representative might say, "Let me share some of my goals for this negotiation. I need to find a way to cover the increasing cost of raw materials, achieve the kind of profit that will allow us to invest in new product development, and better manage inventory as storage costs are becoming less predictable." He didn't just say he needed a high price, but instead shared what he was trying to achieve with that price.

But the representative has other interests he has chosen not to share: He really needs a solid reference to use with other accounts and he wants to set a good price precedent here so that he can use it when selling this new product to another customer. He might share that later in the negotiation, but right now, at the beginning of the negotiation, he is worried (rightly so) that his counterpart could use those interests against him: "Oh, we'd be thrilled to serve as a reference for other customers . . . for a 15% discount."

There is also information here that he would never share: the fact that without this sale, he won't make his quarterly numbers, and that he's already tried to convince every other leading customer in this industry to adopt this new product. Both of these statements would show how weak his alternatives are.

Most often, you don't want to put all of your interests on the table, at least not at the outset. But you want to get enough out there so that your counterpart follows suit.

Capture both sets of interests

Push hard and generate as many interests as possible. During the negotiation, list your interests on a common piece of paper, computer screen, or flip chart so that you can refer to them when you move on to brainstorming options. Don't worry; the whole process is iterative, so you'll still have opportunities to add to or adjust the list of interests later.

Jointly Brainstorm Possible Options

With both parties' interests on the table, imagine solutions that might satisfy all or most of them. This discussion works best when accomplished in two steps: Generate ideas first, and then evaluate and refine them.

Generate options

Before you begin, tell your counterpart that you'd like to move into a joint problem-solving mode and brainstorm together to come up with possibilities, withholding judgment for the time being. Refer to the interests that you captured earlier and ask what you could do to address each one or, better yet, combinations of them. Bring in any options you came up with in your preparation that are still relevant based on the interests you discussed.

Engage your counterpart so that she's also creating possibilities. We've had experienced salespeople tell us that once they have everyone's interests on the table, they throw out a few options and the customer chooses one and they go from there. That's OK, but it would be better to have the customer build off the solutions she's offered and jointly come up with even better options. When you invent ideas together, it's easier to reach an agreement later on because you'll have more options to choose from and you'll feel joint ownership over them.

Focus on generating *possibilities*, not evaluating them, and certainly not eliminating them. The word *possibilities* is important for three reasons:

- First, whatever options you come up with together at this point are just that: possibilities, not offers or commitments. Be clear that you and your counterpart should feel free to come up with ideas even if you can't commit to them. Your options need not be fully formed either; if you want to suggest something without assigning a concrete number to it, it's fine to leave that blank for now.

- Second, the options should be within the realm of what's possible. You don't need to spend a lot of time at this point thinking about whether they're better than your best alternative or if they meet fair standards, however. The options should be possible, but they don't need to be good at this point.

- Third, the "s" is very important: Invent more than one option. If you toss out only one possibility, even if it is creative, it may be heard as an offer rather than one of many options. Throwing out multiple options at once encourages your counterpart to build on your ideas and avoids an unproductive back-and-forth. Offering three or four possibilities increases your chances of iterating together to find a solution that meets both your interests.

As you invent options, you might also discover new interests—yours and your counterpart's. If an option either of you comes up with sounds odd, think about why it might actually make sense and if it reflects an interest you haven't identified yet. Iterating between options and interests and back to options is a good sign that you're being open to the fluid nature of this process.

When you've generated as many options as you can, go back to your lists of interests and check that you have an option that addresses each one.

GENERATING OPTIONS: AN EXAMPLE

Imagine that you and your colleague are negotiating how to allocate a limited budget for next year. You say, "We could split it 50–50." Neither of you is satisfied, so you offer, "Or maybe I could take more of it and compensate you by lending you some needed resources. Or—wait—crazy idea: We could go try to negotiate with Pablo to drop one of his key projects this year and give us some of his budget."

Your colleague thinks for a minute and then adds to your ideas. "Well, maybe that idea isn't so crazy. You or I could also consider dropping a key project and giving the other one the budget for that. Or, since you said one key reason you needed more budget this year was to make investments in that new market you've been pursuing, maybe I could help since we've already started tapping into that market."

This makes sense to you, so you build further on the ideas: "If we went together to discuss with our boss

---

Be prepared for this process to take a while, sometimes multiple sessions. To see how this process of generating options might look in action, see the box "Generating Options: An Example."

Evaluate and refine your options

Once you feel as if you have truly exhausted the options you both can develop and have gone back to your and your

GENERATING OPTIONS: AN EXAMPLE

that either we need to get some more funding or one of us will need to drop a key project, we'd have more power than if one of us went alone. And, I forgot that you already have a small team in that market. Can we make use of some of your people to do some prospecting work for us?"

"I'm not ready to commit," she replies, "but we should be able to work with you part-time or introduce you to some people we're starting to work with in the market."

Because you and your counterpart understood each other's interests and weren't afraid to suggest "crazy" ideas, you were able to come up with a plan that not only works for both of you but may also save the company money. If you'd agreed to the first option—a 50–50 budget split—or spent time haggling over who got what percent, you wouldn't have realized that these opportunities were available.

---

counterpart's lists of interests to see if they spark any new ideas, narrow down your brainstormed list. If there are obvious options that don't meet your or your counterpart's interests well, now is a good time to weed them out.

For example, if you and your customer have developed various options for pricing and payment terms for a project, you might note that two of the options where he pays the bulk of the fee at the end is problematic for you, given that you are hoping to pay for highly specialized engineering resources that you need to subcontract out and pay for up front. He might share that the option in which you get a success bonus for delivering early is interesting, but since he is not funded for that event, he would not be able to pay you in that way.

As you each explain your thinking, you are, of course, not only winnowing down some options, but highlighting some interests that might spark new options. Don't rush to get your list of options down to just one or two yet, but do refine the list to ensure most options are ones that meet your and his interests well.

Use Standards to Narrow Options

Holding an objective yardstick up to your options will help you further improve some and eliminate others, leaving you with few solid options to take forward. Apply standards to make sure that each option would seem fair and reasonable to an unbiased outside party. Also use standards to fill in any gaps in the options, such as what percentage of time your counterpart's team might devote to your projects or what exact price increase you'll ask a customer for.

You already have some standards at your fingertips from your prep work. But now that you better understand the other party's interests and have some real options to work with, brainstorm useful and relevant criteria together. You might prompt your counterpart, "Considering the individuals we will need to explain our agreement to, what kinds of standards might we use to refine and evaluate the options we've come up with?"

Use sources and data that will be the most persuasive to you and the other party. For example, if you are negotiating with a customer, you might share the kinds of deals you have struck with other companies she respects and feels are similar to her company. In the alternative, avoid talking about terms and conditions, or pricing used with customers who purchase a lot less or buy a very different product or service from you. And don't pick standards that favor only your viewpoint. Choose ones that would seem fair whichever side you were on. The goal here is to make sure that any options still on the table are truly defensible to *both* parties.

For larger, more complex negotiations, think about how the deal would come across in a press release describing the final agreement. Draft one to share with the other party so that you both can assess how others would evaluate the option in front of you.

Use standards to support an appealing option

When discussing an option that you believe is a good solution, use a standard to support it. Though the goal here is to persuade the other party to believe that the solution is a valid one, also make it clear that you're bringing up this standard to make sure the final decision is fair and defensible. If you ask your supplier to consider decreasing his price by 10%, for example, you'll be more persuasive if you show that similar suppliers are also decreasing their prices by 8% to 12%. He may not like the decrease, but he'll see that your request isn't arbitrary, and you've given him evidence so that he can go back to the company's stakeholders to discuss the request.

Citing a standard doesn't necessarily mean that the other party will accept it. In the example earlier, the supplier might come back with a persuasive argument about why his company is different from the suppliers who are lowering their prices. Either way, you're now focused on what the right number or term or policy ought to be and the defensible reasons for it, not simply what one party wants it to be.

Use standards to eliminate an unfavorable option

When the other party advocates for an option that you don't feel is fair or defensible, use standards to support your argument against it. Ask your counterpart, "Why that number?" or "On what are you basing that amount?" or, often even more effectively, "How would I justify that figure to my boss?" Have her explain to you why the option is fair or defensible, especially if you have a standard that shows it might not be.

If she can't, suggest a standard that might make sense instead.

Identify and reconcile conflicting standards

Of course, it's very possible that you and your counterpart will bring conflicting standards to the table. Perhaps you found data that shows people in your position get paid an average of $20K more than you do, but your boss says that he has evidence that your salary is on the high end of average. Be sure that you're comparing apples with apples. Perhaps your data assumes that you have an advanced degree, and your boss is looking only at how much programming experience you have and doesn't think a master's in international relations is relevant to your role. Discuss which data is appropriate for your situation.

If this doesn't work, research additional standards on your own that you think might be applicable or helpful, jointly define what you think would make a good standard, or appeal to an unbiased third party who can provide insight on what an appropriate number would be.

If you're truly at an impasse, circle back to your interests and options, and try to get more solutions on the table that could hold up to both your standards.

Be persuasive—and open to persuasion

Applying standards can be tricky because you need to persuade the other party that some options are acceptable (or not). When brandishing a standard, it can be easy to act dismissive or antagonize the person across the table. Be both assertive and empathetic. Remember what you learned about communication and keep reflecting what you've heard back to your counterpart as you ask for more information: "I'm hearing that what you really are interested in is x. Help me understand why that might be fair."

One of the ironies of negotiation is that you're more persuasive if you seem open to persuasion yourself. Don't roll over; that won't help. But listen, consider the other person's point of view, and assume you might have something to learn. As your counterpart sees you do this, she will do the same.

Eventually, by applying standards and iterating and refining the options, you'll arrive at a few workable solutions. The options on the table should meet both of your interests and should be defensible by both parties. Now you move to using your alternatives and commitments to make a good choice among these options.

Chapter 8
Select the Right Outcome

Narrow in on a workable solution and commit with care.

With a few solutions left in front of you, it's time to move toward a final agreement. Do this by applying your alternative and making sure what's on the table is better. Then make commitments carefully so that the agreement is workable for all parties.

Compare Your Options to Alternatives

It's possible, maybe even inevitable, that you and your counterpart will have already stumbled on a discussion of alternatives by this point. As with all of the elements, consider addressing them as they come up in the conversation. But if that hasn't happened yet, now is the time.

Evaluate the remaining options

As we've already discussed, you want a solution that's better than your best alternative. Measure the remaining solutions against this alternative. If one of them passes, you're in good shape. In many negotiations, you never need to share your alternatives with the other party; you silently measure the solution against your best one.

Push for a better solution

If the options left after applying fair standards are not better than your best alternative, use that fact to push you—and your counterpart—to come up with better options.

For example, you could say, "Right now, the options on the table are good, but not nearly as good as what I can do on my own. Is the same true for you?" Or you might say, "For us to reach an agreement, we need to work harder to come up with something better than my team could do elsewhere. Right now I believe I could get 10% more value by going with another vendor, and perhaps as much if we simply used what's left in inventory of your old product."

Be sure to frame the discussion as an effort to do better than your alternative, not as a threat. You might have said, "If you can't do better than what's on the table, I'm going to go with a different vendor," but while threats like these sometimes get the other party to pay attention, most often they derail the negotiation. Your counterpart will likely make her own threat and you'll get stuck in a back-and-forth.

If your alternatives are weak to begin with, you likely will not want to reveal them, no matter the message. In this case, focus all the more on getting creative with your options.

Challenge the Other Party's Alternatives

Remember that even if your own alternatives are weak, the other party's may not be any better. Throughout the negotiation, look for signals of how good your counterpart believes his alternatives to be. You took an educated guess during your prep work, but listen to what he actually says in the negotiation. Watch for clues about what he would do if he had to walk away.

Keep in mind that your counterpart might exaggerate how good his alternatives are. If you suspect that's the case, do some research or even ask some questions to find out how realistic what he's told you is. Does his organization really have other vendors who provide a similar service? Might they truly be able to do it on their own? Can they really wait you out a few quarters until you do what they want?

Furthermore, just because some of these things are possible doesn't mean your counterpart actually wants to see them come to pass. Ask questions that challenge how attractive his alternative is. Can the other vendor his company is considering really meet its volume needs and deliver the same quality you can? What costs would the other party's organization incur doing it themselves? You're not just testing the strength of the other party's alternatives here; you're also making your counterpart see his weaknesses. Educate him: "It can take months to transfer to a new provider when you take into account all of the equipment that needs to be replaced." "The operating life of our competitors' products is two years with no guarantee. Ours, while slightly more expensive, have an operating life of twice that, and we are the only ones who provide a two-year guarantee." This may not change your counterpart's view right away, but it will give him food for thought.

When to walk away

If you still aren't able to identify an option that's better than your best alternative, then you may need to resort to that alternative. That's OK: It's not a failure to walk away if you can't negotiate an agreement that's better. Never negotiate just to agree. Instead of walking away, you may also be able to wait it out until you can develop a stronger alternative or until the other party's weakens. Perhaps you can negotiate with others in your counterpart's organization or find other companies that can meet your needs.

However, if you have successfully come up with solutions that surpass your best alternative, it's time to think about commitments.

Make Commitments Carefully

Now that you have a few strong options left on the table, assess them against the following three criteria to narrow them down further and make sure you should commit.

1. **It's operational and sufficient.** The timeline, terms, and conditions in the given option need

to be realistic and detailed enough to be implemented. Imagine putting the agreement into action, thinking about each step you'd need to take, and make sure you haven't left out anything that still needs to be agreed upon.

2. **You have the authority to commit to it.** Don't get carried away in the room and make agreements you're not allowed to (or let your counterpart do the same). Look at what's about to be agreed to, and think through whether you're allowed to sign on the dotted line or if you need approval from others.

3. **You'll be able to sell it internally to key stakeholders.** Test the solution with the right people before you make any commitment. This may be your boss, upper management, your team, or, in a negotiation that would affect your family, your spouse or children. They may have concerns or ideas you haven't considered.

You can apply these three criteria during the discussion silently, or you might need to step away from the table and talk to others before making a commitment. Either way, devote careful attention to this step. You want to see through what you've agreed to and be sure the other party can do the same.

Leave committing to any options until the very end. Even if you seem to have found options that meet all the criteria, force yourself to stay in the circle a bit longer, inventing and refining, to make sure you've come up with the *best* possible arrangement. Do this whether your negotiation is a five-minute hallway discussion or a months-long formal process. In the same way that you want to start preparing for a negotiation as early as possible, you also want to commit to its outcome as late as you can. As you do, make sure you've avoided the common mistakes in the box "Watch Out for Common Mistakes."

At this point, if all has gone well, you should have a final agreement that meets the seven elements of success.

Of course, not every negotiation goes this smoothly. Every negotiator faces obstacles and struggles, and even in the circle of value, there may be contention. In the next chapter, I'll talk about how to adjust to realities in the room; in the next section, I'll talk about problems people most often encounter and how to handle them.

WATCH OUT FOR COMMON MISTAKES

There are a few places where many negotiators get tripped up when using the circle of value approach. Here are the most common ones to watch out for and avoid:

- **Failing to listen.** When you've put hours or days into your preparation, it makes sense that you want to share your interests, lay out options, and so forth. But when you get into the room, focus on listening and asking questions as much as—if not more than—presenting.

WATCH OUT FOR COMMON MISTAKES

- **Sacrificing your interests in order to preserve the relationship.** Deal with the relationship separately. Resolve any trust issues before you move on to the substance of the negotiation.

- **Focusing on positions, not interests.** It's easy to get wrapped up in what you or the other party wants and move too quickly into the specifics of the potential agreements. But unless you both understand the drivers behind your positions, you won't be able to find an agreement that satisfies both parties' interests.

- **Evaluating options too soon.** When your counterpart throws out an option that's not appealing to you, don't start pointing out what's wrong with it. Spend time coming up with many options together before you start criticizing.

- **Using your best alternative as your only bar for success.** Your goal shouldn't be doing "well enough." Press for more options that meet your interests better and apply real standards so that you don't accept an offer that is too low. It might be tempting to agree to a 5% raise simply because it's better than your current salary, but if others with your talent are getting 8% and 10% increases, then you're leaving value on the

WATCH OUT FOR COMMON MISTAKES

table that you can capture with more work and discipline.

- **Committing too early in the process.** Your counterpart may suggest an option early on that sounds perfect to you and is based on a very reasonable standard. Don't jump on it, though. Agreeing to one suggestion prematurely will limit creativity. Be patient and take time to act thoughtfully and carefully. You may come up with an even better option.

Chapter 9
Continuously Adapt Your Approach

Be prepared to change course.

One of the things many negotiators find frustrating is the fact that you can't control what the other party does. All of the preparation you've done will help you shape and direct the process, and the circle of value approach will optimize your chances of working together toward a joint solution, but the reality is that you don't know what your counterpart will say, do, propose, or reject—or in what order. It's therefore important to be flexible when you're in the room.

Here are several ways to stay nimble and adjust your approach when necessary.

Role-Play

When you're between negotiation sessions and not sure in what direction to go, or you want to feel more confident implementing your planned approach, it's helpful to practice with someone else before going back into the room with your counterpart. Seeing and feeling the approach in action helps you decide whether or not you're on the right course.

Practicing your approach

Maybe you haven't been able to get your counterpart to discuss interests or your attempt to negotiate on two tracks doesn't seem to be working. Maybe you're not sure how to begin brainstorming options in your next session or you're uncomfortable presenting the standards you want to bring to the table. Ask a colleague to play the role of your counterpart as you test out what you might say and do. If possible, choose someone who doesn't have a stake in the outcome of the negotiation so that she can be objective. If you have to work with someone who is directly involved, pick someone who you know will be honest with you.

Explain the situation to her, perhaps even sharing your preparation tool so that she can orient herself, and then try out different approaches. Play it out multiple times. Ask for feedback after each try. "How did that sound? How did that feel? Was that persuasive?" Adjust your approach and repeat.

Your colleague might even make some suggestions. "What if you tried sharing a few more of your interests first or explained why you are asking about that there?" Keep practicing. When you feel comfortable—and have a range of moves you can use—you're ready to go back to the table.

Understanding your counterpart

If you're struggling to understand why your counterpart is behaving in a certain way, try a role reversal: You play your counterpart and ask a trusted colleague to play you. Before you begin, have your colleague interview you (being yourself) so that he can begin to understand how you think, what you feel, and what things you've been saying and doing in the negotiation. This will also allow him to accurately play your role when you're ready.

Next, have your colleague interview you again, this time with you playing your counterpart, so that you can begin to feel, think, speak, and act the way she does. Keep doing this until you really feel and speak like her.

Then, negotiate: your colleague as you, and you as your counterpart. After a few minutes, stop and review: What did you learn about your counterpart by getting inside her head? Do you better understand her perspective? Perhaps you have a better sense of why she has been acting the way she has.

Consider what you learned about the impact of your own words (spoken by your colleague). Are you being persuasive? Is your counterpart likely hearing what you're trying to say? Ask your colleague for observations as well.

Make adjustments to your approach. Perhaps you could be more persuasive on certain points or maybe you need to be more empathetic to build trust.

Become a Fly on the Wall

Any good athlete knows how to hop off the field or the court for a moment and assess what's going on. She becomes a "fly on the wall," stepping out of the action briefly to observe what she, her teammates, and her opponent are doing. Successful athletes adjust their approach (or consciously choose to stick to it) given what they see, and jump back into the game and execute.

A good negotiator has the same skill. Throughout the negotiation, pop out of the action and look at what's happening. Narrate to yourself what's taking place: "She has explained her interests. I shared mine. Now we're moving into options. Is this going smoothly? If not, I could stay with interests a bit longer, or I could move to standards next, or I could even ask for a time-out." Avoid getting stuck in your narrow view of the situation so that you can adjust as necessary.

Ideally you'll be able to do this yourself while at the table, but you can also assign people on your team to monitor certain slices of the negotiation. For example, you might ask Bob to watch how the other party reacts to certain options and Joan to monitor how your counterpart responds to messages you're sending.

Take an Occasional Break

If you have trouble becoming a fly on the wall in the heat of the negotiation, consider asking for a brief pause in the discussion. Don't hesitate to request a break if you're not sure what to do next, if you get annoyed and need time to calm down, or if you want to consult with colleagues who aren't at the table. Also consider asking for a time-out if you learn something unexpected or are truly surprised.

A break could be 10 minutes or it could be a few days. You can explain the reason for the time away from the table, or, if you're concerned about sending the wrong signal to your counterpart, you can always ask for a chance to use the restroom, check your e-mail, or grab a cup of coffee.

It's often less awkward if you establish up front that either of you can call a break at any time. That way it doesn't look odd if you ask for a time-out right after your counterpart has suggested an option you especially don't like, or if you head to the restroom when you're stumped about which standards to apply.

Conduct Frequent Reviews and Make Corrections

A smart negotiator also takes a more complete step back at certain points to review what's happening in the negotiation. Do this frequently—after each negotiation session to update prep documents, anytime you're stuck or things get heated, and prior to making any commitments.

At each of these junctures, ask yourself what's working and what you might do differently. Even if you only do this in your head for 10 minutes while driving home, you'll learn something and generate concrete ideas for adjusting your approach.

If you're stuck, do a more formal review, preferably with a colleague or two who can ask you tough questions:

"What did you say right before they threatened to walk away? What led you to say that? Why do you think they might have reacted that way?"

When you're preparing to commit, ask your colleagues to walk through the seven elements for a good outcome. "Does this truly meet your full range of critical interests very well? How many options did you consider? Why do you think this is the best one? Is it truly better than your best alternative?"

Then make any necessary adjustments. Perhaps you need to spend more time coming up with options or focus more on repairing the relationship before you talk about interests. If things aren't moving forward, consider a change of venue, timeline, or even players. Can you bring in someone from your or your counterpart's side who can help?

Don't think of midcourse corrections as failures; it's not uncommon that you'd have to make changes as the negotiation progresses (in fact, it likely means you are truly learning things along the way). Expect to make these kinds of shifts to move the discussion in the right direction and reach a more successful agreement.

Section 3
The Common Challenges

Tools and techniques you can use in specific situations.

All the advice we've given you so far optimizes your chances of reaching a successful agreement. But even with diligent preparation and a thoughtful approach, sometimes the most flexible negotiators can still find themselves stuck.

The four most common problems that negotiators may face are:

1. **There are multiple parties involved.** With numerous people at the table, the complexity of the negotiation has slowed it down or stopped it altogether.

2. **Your counterpart is a hard bargainer.** Your fellow negotiator resists your attempts to work collaboratively and instead states a position and demands concessions.

3. **Communication breaks down.** You and the other party keep talking past each other, unable to understand each other's perspectives, never mind reach an agreement.

4. **The conversation gets heated.** Emotions run high and either you or your counterpart is upset, angry, or offended.

In the chapters that follow, I'll explain how to overcome each of these issues in turn.

Chapter 10
Align Multiple Parties

Avoid inefficiency and chaos.

The Problem

Many negotiations involve more than two parties, all of whom need to subscribe to a final agreement. These are situations in which there aren't just multiple stakeholders behind the scenes, but also multiple parties sitting at the table: Perhaps you're negotiating the details of a go-to-market strategy with multiple channel partners; maybe you work for a research institution that is collaborating with several others on a government contract; or perhaps you're working on a complex services sale that involves a number of individuals from both the customer's and your organizations. When you have more than two parties that want to agree on a final solution, the circle of value approach becomes more complicated.

Why It Happens

There are two primary reasons that these negotiations are more complex:

- **People overload.** Getting the parties to commit to an option or agreement typically takes longer simply because there are more individuals involved. Start by discussing agenda items and ground rules at the beginning of the negotiation. You can also try to make things easier by identifying who the decision makers are and leaving everyone else out of the mix, but that can backfire if you find out later that there are others who need to have a voice as well.

- **Process complexity.** Negotiating with multiple parties means you have more interests to meet, more options to sort through, and more alternatives to consider.

Balancing the need to include and consult many different parties with the reality of how long it may take to consider all the options that satisfy their interests is not easy.

What to Do About It

There are ways to accelerate the process and still make sure that all points of view are considered.

Make it clear who decides

You can work through complex decisions more efficiently—and avoid confusion and frustration—by establishing expectations up front about who gets to decide what.

People have different interests in the negotiation, so they should play different roles in making a final decision. Those roles fall into three categories:

- **Inform.** Those who need to know about a decision and its rationale but don't need to (and likely, when pressed, don't really want to) be involved in the negotiation itself. This broad category of people includes those who have to implement the agreement or are otherwise affected by it, but don't have particular expertise or viewpoints needed in the discussion itself. For example, the vast majority of end users of a new product or service being purchased would fall into this category.

- **Consult.** Those whose input should inform the decision. These are the advisers to the decision makers. Consider their needs or advice before making a decision, though ultimately they don't need or get a vote. These participants typically have a unique perspective or expertise that you want to draw upon.

- **Negotiate.** Those who are ultimately responsible for all or key parts of the final agreement. These are people who need to make the decision because of their position, roles, responsibilities, or authority. It can be helpful to subdivide this group into those who have veto power (the agreement cannot go forward without their consent) and those who can simply vote on an issue (the group can proceed without their approval if necessary).

It's best to formally establish these roles early in the negotiation, ideally in advance of sitting down together or when you first get in the room. At the very least, you want to have a discussion about roles before you begin refining options.

To decide who goes in which category:

1. **List each decision that will need to be made.**
   When you were preparing for the negotiation, you laid out the various issues that needed to be addressed in a negotiation. Using those, make a list of the specific decisions that need to be made.

2. **Assign each person a role for each decision.**
   Identify all the parties who have a stake in each decision and place them in one of the three buckets: Inform, Consult, or Negotiate (veto/vote). Keep in mind that the same person might be in different buckets for different decisions; your boss might have veto rights on the decision about pricing but needs to be consulted only about the length of the service contract. Use a chart like the one in table 10-1 to capture this work.

   You may be tempted to put most people in the "Negotiate" category, but that's not realistic, and many of them don't actually need or want to be that closely involved. Instead, aim to put each person in the bucket as far to the left side as

TABLE 10-1

Assigning negotiation roles

Decision	Inform	Consult	Negotiate—Has a Vote	Negotiate—Has a Veto
Product Pricing	**Seller:** Sales Representatives, Product Representatives **Buyer:** Business Unit Manager	**Seller:** Product Manager, Account Executive **Buyer:** Procurement Lead, Finance Lead	**Seller:** VP of Pricing, Finance Lead **Buyer:** VP of Procurement	**Seller:** SVP of Sales **Buyer:** Business Unit General Manager
Level of Product Support	**Both companies:** Finance	**Seller:** Service Line Leads **Buyer:** Procurement VP and Lead **Both companies:** Legal	**Seller:** Head of Sales **Buyer:** Business Unit General Manager	**Seller:** VP of Services **Buyer:** Business Unit VP of Quality

possible, limiting those in this crucial group to those who really must be there.

3. **Share and get feedback.** Be clear with everyone about the role you expect them to play and why. Ask for their input. Negotiate as necessary with people over their roles, and get their commitment to honor them during the negotiation.

    Sometimes people will easily fall into these roles, and other times it will take some discussion. If there is disagreement, discuss why the person feels she needs to be in the role she's requesting. Is she truly prepared to put in the effort and time necessary? Can a different role meet her interests? For example, you might say something like, "You had said you want to be in the Negotiate role because you want to share your opinion on the risks here. Could that be achieved in the Consult role, especially since your boss is already in the Negotiate role?"

This process can add work to your negotiation, but it will also help streamline the decision-making process, ultimately saving time.

Get people on the same page—literally

Even with agreed-upon responsibilities, it can be difficult to get everyone in a multiparty situation to agree to a solution.

Often each party will simply present their ideal solution and wait for the other parties to react or add more detail. This can jump-start a long, unproductive game of positional bargaining that leads to a lowest-common-denominator solution. Even if you don't fall into these traps and manage to draft a single proposal and circulate it to others for feedback, sorting through their reactions can descend into chaos.

Instead, use what we call the *one-text procedure*. As its name suggests, this process forces everyone to focus on one draft of an agreement. The parties work together on that single shared document, seeking to improve it along the way by offering criticism (not suggestions), allowing the drafter to creatively edit the draft from one round of feedback to the next.

Here's how it works:

1. **Choose a drafter.** Work together to select one individual who will be solely responsible for all writing and editing. Find someone who is known to be respected and trusted, a good listener, and creative. Look for a person who has built enough credibility with everyone at the table to be considered neutral. Ideally, he'll have no direct stake in the decision but understand the context and the issues. If everyone can't agree on who should play this role, create a small team composed of representatives from each party. You can also use an uninvolved outsider.

   If you're unable to find someone for this role, you may decide that you are the best person to draft the agreement. If this is the case, be very clear throughout the process which hat you're wearing when; at times, you will be the balanced facilitator soliciting and capturing feedback from others, while at other times, you will play the role of critiquing your own draft. No matter what, you'll need to take a fair, balanced approach to the discussion and to the drafting, understanding that you can't just focus on your own interests.

2. **Listen to each party's views.** The drafter then elicits interests from each party. He may do this in separate interviews or while everyone is together in the room. Each side is likely to make the case for what the solution should be, but it's the drafter's responsibility to ask questions that get at the interests underlying the preferred solutions and current positions. The drafter will want to probe deeply, asking, "Why?" "For what purpose?" and "What are you trying to achieve (or avoid)?"

3. **Create a rough draft.** The drafter then creates a rough solution that is impartial and responsive to what he's heard. It should be clear that this is a draft and not final in any way. Driving that point home can be as simple as writing "draft for discussion only" on each page.

4. **Ask for criticism.** The drafter shares the one text, asking each party in what ways the current draft does not meet their interests. Usually in this first round, he asks them as a group, as it is helpful for each participant to hear the others' answers. The drafter should not defend or explain the draft.

Instead, he asks questions like, "What would be wrong with something like this?" "Which interests of yours are not reasonably met with this proposal?" If he gets back a suggestion ("You should just change that term, and I will be set"), he should always ask about the interests behind it ("Why might that make more sense than what is there?"). His tone should not be defensive, but inquisitive.

Capitalizing on people's natural willingness to criticize, this approach further exposes their underlying interests. Ideally, the drafter will record all of those new interests heard in a place where everyone can see them. (See the box "Questions to Ask in the One-Text Procedure.")

5. **Make revisions.** The drafter then refines the text. He looks for new creative solutions, ideas that reconcile differences, and ways to create joint gains. If he believes certain interests are still not being shared, he might even put in a controversial idea or a few to spur criticism in the next round. The drafter should do this transparently, by noting what he has done and why. He again marks it as a "draft" and brings it back to the negotiators.

6. **Repeat.** The drafter once again asks all parties for their criticism, probing for interests, testing them, recording them, and digging more deeply for what is driving any proposed change. Most often this is done in live sessions, but if necessary,

he might send out a draft with numbered lines and ask the negotiating parties to write up their feedback in a separate document. Some individuals might beg to mark their changes directly on the draft, but the drafter should not give in. The result would be too many unreconciled versions, and all those productive steps toward one organized solution would be lost.

In this next round, the drafter gathers up the criticism, shares his appreciation with the negotiators, and goes back to improve the draft on his own. He then continues to alternate between soliciting criticism and revising. He continues iterating this way until he believes he cannot make the draft any better, the benefits of further improvement seem not worth the cost in time and effort, or he runs out of time.

7. **Present a choice.** At this point, the drafter presents all parties with a stark choice: Accept the draft as is or accept the consequences of not coming to an agreement. He might say something like:

    "I have done the very best I can. I can't promise everyone will be 100% happy, but I've listened to all of you and tried hard to meet many of your underlying interests. This is a final proposal. I don't think we can make it any better. If you all say yes, then we have ourselves an agreement. If you say no, we may all have to revert to our best alternative. I now need a simple yes or no from each of you."

QUESTIONS TO ASK IN THE ONE-TEXT PROCEDURE

- What is wrong with this draft as it is presented now?

- Do you have important interests that this draft does not adequately address? Which ones? Why are they important?

- What else seems wrong or is missing from the draft? Why are these things important?

- Do you have other ideas for improvement? What are your reasons for suggesting these items? What key unmet interests do they address?

- Do you have other ideas for how conflicting interests might be creatively and fairly resolved?

- Understanding why you would like this particular interest met, but given that it has become clear that it is in direct conflict with others' interests, why should meeting your interest here take priority over meeting theirs? What standards or fair process might we apply to deciding this?

My colleagues and I have used the one-text procedure in complex multiparty situations, such as peace negotiations, complex sales, mergers and acquisitions, and large-scale organizational change initiatives, and seemingly straightforward discussions, such as who gets which office, how a new policy should read, how to set budgets for the next fiscal year, and even where to go on vacation with the extended family.

The process leads to much better outcomes and builds relationships. Despite the number of people involved, people have a voice, they feel heard, and they begin to view crafting an agreement as a joint problem.

While the process as a whole may seem like it would take longer than putting everyone in a room and letting them fight it out, that approach usually just leads to deadlock or forced compromises that themselves often lead to unworkable agreements that can't be implemented properly. In the end, the one-text approach often saves time.

This process works very well for situations in which there are multiple parties at the table, but it can also be helpful for one-on-one negotiations in which you know your counterpart is going to have to vet the agreement with an array of internal constituents. You might develop a rough draft together, and then she can run the one-text procedure inside her organization. Of course, you have interests that need to be met, too, so remain involved to ensure your interests are taken into account in future drafts.

Negotiating with many individuals who have widely disparate interests can be daunting, but clarifying decision-making roles and using the one-text procedure is a disciplined way to bring all those voices together to reach one solution.

Chapter 11
Tame the Hard Bargainer

Shift the conversation.

The Problem

You've worked hard to prepare for the negotiation, and you're ready to enter the circle of value. But every time you try to better understand your counterpart's interests or jointly brainstorm options, he resists. Rather than following your approach, he's wedded to using typical negotiation tactics: laying out his position, making threats, and waiting for you to make concessions. He dismisses your questions about what's driving his demands, saying instead, "That's not relevant. I want what I want."

Take, for example, Ruben, a salesperson trying to sell a large piece of equipment to George, his potential customer. George makes an opening demand: "I'm going to need a 10% discount." He explains that none of his other suppliers would get away with charging more, not even his top suppliers. When Ruben asks George why, explaining that he wants to understand his underlying interests, George cuts him off. "Listen, I'm doing you a favor because I like working with you. If this were someone else, I'd ask for an even steeper discount." He adds, "If you were a good partner, you'd give us this discount. Just remember, my boss is an old friend of your boss, and he can call him anytime."

This kind of answer is frustrating, but panicking, reacting in kind, walking out—or even worse, just giving in—won't get you anywhere. George, as a hard bargainer, is playing a kind of game. Don't get lured into playing the game yourself; it often leads to a compromised solution and a strained relationship.

Why It Happens

You're in this uncomfortable situation because no matter how good your intentions or how well prepared you are, you can't demand that your counterpart negotiate the way you want. There are many reasons people choose to use the unproductive tactics George is using here:

- **This is the only approach they know.** They may assume that this is how negotiations are supposed to be done. If this is the case, you can sometimes show or teach them a better way.

- **This has worked for them in the past.** When they've played the hard bargainer before, they may have been rewarded by previous counterparts who have given concessions and let them "win." Here, too, you may need to show them a more productive approach and make it clear that you're not going to continue to reward their bad behavior.

- **They've been told to negotiate this way by a boss or other superior.** It's possible that someone in their organization pays them to negotiate this way (for example, gives a bonus based on the discount they achieve) or gives them positional instructions, such as "Go get a 10% discount," with no explanation of why or for what purpose. Or perhaps the hard bargainer has seen someone she respects negotiate this way. You don't know what pressure they're under, but you can show them that they might get a better result using a different process.

- **They aren't prepared to negotiate any other way.** They haven't thought through what their interests are, what they might do if they can't reach an agreement, who needs to approve an agreement, and so forth. Give them time to regroup and guidance on how to prepare.

Considering why your counterpart is driving a hard bargain can help you determine how best to respond.

What to Do About It

Your job in this situation is to spot "the game," diagnose what's going on, and then change the tone and direction of the conversation so that you don't mimic your counterpart's style.

Don't react

The first step is to use the skills we talked about in chapter 9 and become a "fly on the wall." Instead of panicking or reacting to threats or demands, take a deep breath, mentally pop out of the negotiation, and objectively look at what's happening. Take a calm, disciplined approach so that you can systematically and strategically decide how to move forward.

Diagnose what's happening

Seek to understand what's going on by using the seven elements to spot the "game" and assess what "moves" your counterpart is making. Determine which of the elements he's using and how he's using them—and, importantly, which elements he's not.

Sometimes you'll see that he's using the elements, but in ways that aren't ideal; he's actually *mis*using them. Where you're trying to brainstorm options that meet both parties' interests, he's pressing for options that meet only his. Where you share very concrete standards based on research and analysis, he might toss out a fuzzy generalization such as, "Everyone agrees to those terms these days." Where you try to build the relationship, he might hold the relationship hostage by making threats if you don't give in.

Let's return to the large equipment sales example from earlier. George made the following four moves:

1. "I'm going to need a 10% discount."

2. "None of our suppliers would get away with charging more."

3. "I'm doing you a favor because I like working with you" and "If you were a good partner, you'd give us this discount."

4. "My boss is an old friend of your boss, and he can call him anytime."

Thinking of the elements, Ruben should note:

- With Move #1, George used commitment to demand that Ruben agree to his position.

- With Move #2, he tossed out just one, very general standard, without supporting it with evidence, and implied that Ruben should take his word for it.

- With Move #3, he tried to use the relationship to get Ruben to make a concession and perhaps even threaten the relationship if he doesn't.

- With Move #4, George is focused on alternatives, sharing that he has a pretty good one and that he can easily exercise it if Ruben doesn't cooperate.

Ruben should also note that George didn't address the other three elements: interests, options, or communication. Now he knows what elements are in play (and which aren't) and how they're being used.

Lastly, consider, too, how you may be contributing to the unhealthy dynamic. What is your body language saying? What's your tone of voice? How did you frame what you shared or asked? Are you acting defensive? Have you responded to his demand with a counter-demand? You can't expect him to exhibit collaborative behaviors if you aren't.

Change the game

Now that you know what's happening, you can work to change it. Here are three approaches you can use:

1. **Introduce an element your counterpart is not using.** Bringing in another element often helps move the conversation forward. If your counterpart is focused on her alternative and keeps pushing you to come to a final resolution, consider presenting some new options, asking about her interests, sharing standards that would allow you to both defend yourselves to relevant stakeholders, and so on.

    In the sales example earlier, Ruben could bring in one of the following elements George has not used:

    *   **Interests.** George wasn't forthcoming about his interests, but Ruben needs to persevere. He should ask why George wants the 10% discount a number of times in a variety of different ways. Why 10%? Why not 8% or 12%? How will George use this extra money?

        If this tack does not work, Ruben should test his own hypotheses about what George's interests might be. Is he trying to improve the margins on his product into which these parts go? Is he trying to fund another project? Does he need to save money to invest in training and support? Alternatively, he could share some of his interests to prime the pump.

- **Options.** Ruben could also say, "Let's consider 10% as one possibility. What are three other ways we could structure this deal?" Or, even better, he could bring in George's interests as well: "I'm guessing the 10% is being driven by your increased production costs, and if so, I can imagine these three other ways we might structure this deal to address that problem."

2. **Take an element your counterpart _is_ using and use it in a different way.** For example, Ruben might recognize George's invocation of his alternative and decide to stay focused on that element. Instead of threatening George with his own alternatives, Ruben can push George on how good his alternative really is. Ruben might ask George what it would look like if he had to go back and get his boss involved, or he could share with George that he's already discussed this deal with his own boss, and any call to his boss would just get directed back to him. He could possibly even remind him of the cost to George's company if the deal falls apart (for example, the costs of switching to a competitor's product).

   Ruben could also note that both of them have good alternatives and then steer the conversation in a different direction: "We both have alternatives, so let's see if we can come up with some better options, and then we can each go back and decide if what we created is better or worse than our alternatives."

Last, Ruben could continue with one of the other elements that George invoked:

- **Standards.** Ruben might inquire into George's suggestion that other potential partners would accept a lower price. He could ask which other suppliers provide a 10% discount or ask if George has *ever* purchased from a supplier who didn't provide such a discount. Any of these questions might be persuasive in and of themselves, or they might lead to a conversation about what standards George would need to persuade his constituents that he was getting a good deal.

- **Commitment.** Ruben could test George's authority to go below 10% and consider trading an immediate commitment to a 5% discount for an agreement to "sign" today. While not a move back into the circle, this exception could be a useful game-changing move. Ruben could ask who in George's organization could commit to something less than 10% and explore how to get that person to the table, or arm George with the arguments he needs to get approval.

- **Relationship.** Finally, Ruben could tell George that he likes doing business with him, too, and that the appropriate discount (if any) to apply here has nothing to do with their relationship and more to do with both sides being treated fairly. Or he might ask if there's anything straining the relationship now (short of price) and address those issues head on, before moving back to how they both determine what a fair price should be.

3. **Call your counterpart out on the game she's playing.** Explicitly say what she's doing, explain the downsides of the tactic she's using, and suggest the circle of value approach instead. You might say something like, "I notice that you're making a unilateral demand, and it seems you'd like me to make a concession in return. That feels like a losing game for both of us. If we put our heads together, we could come up with a solution that would be a lot more valuable to both of us." Don't force a new process down her throat, though; ask: "What would be your concerns about that approach?" Stepping back and explicitly negotiating over the process itself can be a powerful move to refocus the discussion.

To change the game, you'll likely need to use a combination of these three approaches. Which you lead with depends on your unique situation, but often it is easiest to go to an element that isn't being used. Bringing in something new can breathe fresh air into a tense conversation.

Some negotiators have an element or two with which they feel particularly comfortable, so you might go with that element first. There isn't one right move. Rather, think of the seven elements as seven options to choose from whenever you get stuck.

Whichever move you decide to make, persevere. If your first attempt doesn't work, try again. Your first question, "Why do you need 10%?" may not be answered, so ask it again in different ways. If that move does not work, then try one of the other six elements. The good news is that you have seven different places to go, and if you stay focused and disciplined, you'll make progress.

When you can't change the game

On rare occasions, you may simply not be able to change the game. This happens most frequently when your counterpart has an actual interest in being a hard bargainer. For example, he takes some delight in seeing who will back down first or making concessions back and forth. If you have truly exhausted the strategies without success, you have a few choices.

1. Play the game, but play it better than he does. For example, if you are going to engage in the horse-trading game of positional bargaining, be well prepared on all seven elements, keep your measure of success in view, and use this to get the upper hand in his game. For example, use prepared standards to reinforce your positions, brainstormed options to select and use low-cost concessions as you extract high-cost ones from him, and so forth. Keep in mind, though, that you should do this only on very rare occasions. Even if you succeed, you risk setting a bad precedent.

2. Resort to your best alternative, but do so in a way that leaves the door open for the other party

to come back to the table later. You might say, "I wish we could make this work, but as is, I'd simply do better losing this deal than agreeing to it. I have a number of other customers and think it would be better if I focus my attention there. If things change for you, I'd be thrilled if you gave me a call." Sometimes your counterpart won't call, but other times he'll realize his best alternative wasn't quite as good as he thought, is going nowhere, or worse yet, is leading to bad results, and your phone will ring.

Changing the game can save a negotiation that is going nowhere. It often sets a good precedent for future interactions, too. For example, if you bring in a standard that works against a tough negotiator, you've done two things: first, you've established a criterion you both can agree on and point to in the future, and second, you've made it clear that you want to negotiate fairly, rather than using one-sided power plays. Create the history you want to repeat.

This all may sound easier said than done, but armed with the advice here and some practice, you too will be able to do this. Start by watching tough negotiations and thinking about how you would steer your counterpart away from the hard bargainer's tactics. Then practice on some low-risk negotiations, gradually building your way up. As you get more experienced, make sure each time that you step back, diagnose, and make active choices about how you want to reshape the conversation.

Chapter 12
When Communication Breaks Down

Build understanding.

The Problem

Sometimes when you get in the room, you find that you and your counterpart can't get on the same page. Perhaps the conversation has turned contentious quickly, and your counterpart was offended by something you said, even though you didn't mean it that way. Maybe you don't understand why the options that you've suggested don't work for the other party. Or perhaps you find yourselves debating over how you each see the situation or issues in the negotiation. No matter what you do, there seems to be a disconnect.

Take this example from an R&D joint venture between an automobile manufacturer and a producer of electric car parts. Alfredo, one of the executives with the manufacturer, tried to persuade Deirdre, his counterpart with the electronics producer, to move the venture's main site to the Midwest, where the manufacturing of the vehicles took place. Deirdre was resistant, so Alfredo went out of his way to explain the benefits: They would have access to more-talented engineers, and the whole venture would be closer to "where the action was." Every time they spoke and he indicated another benefit, she'd shoot him down. Despite the fact that he had a counterargument ready for every issue she raised—like the fact that they'd save more in the cost of operations than what they'd have to spend on the relocation—still she said no, but would never explain why.

Their relationship was getting strained, since Alfredo simply couldn't understand where Deirdre was coming from, and he was beginning to assume that she was just being difficult. Further proof of this was her odd reaction to something he had said weeks earlier. In trying to be a helpful partner, he had told her proudly that the engineers at his company had finally come up with a method to integrate her company's very complex components into all their car models. He thought she'd be thrilled by this development. Instead, she glared at him and stomped off.

Despite Alfredo's best intentions, several common breakdowns in communication are evident here: Deirdre won't tell Alfredo why his proposals won't work for her; Alfredo has managed to offend Deirdre without knowing why; and Alfredo hasn't created an option that takes Deirdre's perspective and her interests into account.

Why It Happens

Breakdowns in communication aren't an infrequent occurrence in negotiations. To understand why, think about the classic black-and-white drawing that to some people looks like a young girl and, to others, like an old woman. It's the same picture, but people simply see it differently. These are called *partisan perceptions*, and they apply to negotiations the same way. You see the whole negotiation differently—the very act of the negotiation, one another, and the issues at hand.

These perceived differences are dangerous because we often amplify them in our minds. Research has shown that we have a tendency to enhance our own side of an issue—to think of it as more honest or real—while vilifying others into "the opposition." This often leads to negative perceptions of the other party and their reasoning, behavior, or position.

The gaps between your stories can be hard to fill. But if you don't explore the difference together, you're likely to be left debating conclusions instead of reducing conflict and solving problems.

What to Do About It

You can bridge this gap by building mutual understanding. This starts with you: Figure out what information you are lacking and how to get it. After all, you can't change someone's mind unless you know where his mind is. Once you do, you have a better chance of working together to form a solution that works for both of you.

Make understanding a collaborative effort

It helps to acknowledge that partisan perceptions exist and to assume that you will encounter them as a matter of course. When you do, you'll have to deliberately seek to understand your counterpart's perspective, and have that person understand yours:

1. **Ask her to share her reasoning.** Ask questions until you fully understand the other party's story and can see how she would've reached her conclusion (though you don't have to agree with it). Focus on the data she's using to reach conclusions and make clear how you're interpreting the data to reach *your* conclusions.

2. **Repeat it.** Tell your counterpart's story back to her. Test it, and demonstrate that you understand it. If she tells you that you missed something, play back what you learned.

3. **Share *your* story.** Don't present it as an airtight case, but explain how you got to your conclusion so that she understands your reasoning. Openly admit that it's possible that you might not have all the facts and that there may be other legitimate ways to view the situation.

4. **Invite your counterpart to ask questions.** She might ask about your story and how it leads to your conclusion, or she might critique it.

Stay away from the question of who's right. Use this method to get away from "agreeing to disagree" and move toward a mutual understanding of how and why you disagree and building trust.

If you expect partisan perceptions to be particularly divergent in your negotiation, consider discussing them early on in the negotiation process.

Manage impact, not intent

If your counterpart feels offended or hurt by something you said, but you didn't mean it that way, that may be another symptom of a communication breakdown. As someone who didn't mean to offend, it's natural to focus on correcting your counterpart's perception and demonstrating what you *did* intend to say. But your intentions shouldn't be the focus here. Instead, address the impact you might have had.

Begin by exploring the emotions your counterpart is feeling as a result of what you did or said. If he is not forthcoming about his feelings, test what you think your impact might have been: "While it was not my intent, I fear what I did yesterday ended up putting you in an embarrassing situation with your boss," or "I am truly worried that what I said sounded like I was criticizing your team, when I didn't mean to." Open up the conversation, explore unintended results, and let him talk. Show empathy or at least understanding, and never hesitate to apologize. You are not apologizing for good intent; you are apologizing for the impact.

Consider the example in which Alfredo's intent was to share how he had helped Deirdre and her company.

Unfortunately, from her reaction, Alfredo could tell that Deirdre hadn't understood it that way. What Alfredo didn't know was that Deirdre had heard many times how much better the engineering talent was at Alfredo's company than at hers. So based on her own experience, she heard one-upmanship and boasting—and, in effect, criticism. She was hurt by being reminded of what she failed to accomplish.

But Alfredo did not know that; to him, her reaction was baffling. Alfredo's next step was to follow up with Deirdre, explaining that he had expected a different reaction and asking her what was wrong. Still angry, Deirdre accused him of insulting her and showing off. But Alfredo kept asking questions about her reaction. When she calmed down, Deirdre explained how she had understood his remark and the background behind her reaction. She explained that she had always seen her failure to create an easier-to-use product as a pivotal moment in her career, and she hadn't been truly happy with her job since. Alfredo then had the opportunity to respond, "I can imagine how that makes you feel. I'm so sorry for bringing it all up and hurting you."

By managing the negative impact of what he had said, rather than insisting that Deirdre understand his intent, Alfredo learned more about Deirdre's interests, which then helped him in the course of his negotiation with her: She was competitive, she wished she could solve her company's problems, and she wanted to improve her job. He also gained Deirdre's trust; he put the relationship back on track by asking questions, listening carefully, and acknowledging the impact of his words and the validity of Deirdre's feelings.

Create a "yesable" proposition

If your counterpart keeps saying no to your proposals and options and you can't understand why, that's also a sign of miscommunication. While it's easy to assume that the person is being irrational or stubborn, neither conclusion is helpful nor, most often, true. People do what they think is in their best interests, whether we understand those interests or not.

Alfredo already shared with Deirdre all the reasons the move makes sense to him and explained away every concern she raised. It was unlikely he would get anywhere by continuing to try to persuade her.

Instead, after their conversation, Alfredo realized that his proposal must not meet Deirdre's interests well. Instead of continuing to press her, he stepped into her shoes to try to better understand *why* his idea wasn't winning her over. His goal was to uncover which of her interests weren't being met and to brainstorm new options that might work better for her.

My partner Roger Fisher always advised people to think about the decision from the other party's point of view and to use this to craft a *yesable proposition*. To create a yesable proposition in your negotiation, follow these five steps:

1. **Ask yourself whether you're trying to persuade the right person.** Sometimes the person with

whom you're negotiating may be saying no because the options don't satisfy other key parties. This could indicate that you should negotiate with someone else, or it might simply mean that you need to keep in mind that your counterpart will later need to get buy-in from someone else. In either case, you need to analyze the interests of these outside stakeholders and even get them directly involved in the discussion. For example, Alfredo might have talked to Deirdre's boss instead if he had realized that Deirdre didn't have the authority to make the decision whether to move the venture.

2. **Imagine what choice your counterpart believes you're asking her to make.** Think about how your counterpart might describe that choice to herself from her perspective, not yours. Alfredo, for example, might realize that he has been thinking about the question in Deirdre's mind as, "Shall I finally agree to Alfredo's excellent proposal to create closer collaboration, more efficiency, and lower operating costs for me?" when she's really thinking something more like, "Shall I today give in to another demand from superstar Alfredo, have to lay people off in one location only to have to hire people in the new location, and have people from his company more easily poke their noses into our business?"

     Imagining this tougher and not very appealing choice for Deirdre would help Alfredo realize more of her interests and come up with new options that meet them.

3. **Make a list of the negative consequences the other party might perceive in saying yes to the current proposal.** Carefully gauge what would happen for your counterpart if she said yes to your proposal. Make a list of the potential negative outcomes. (Put the positives aside for now; you've already tried to use those to convince her, and they haven't worked.) Then, make a separate list of reasons it would *benefit* her to say no to you. Put yourself in her shoes. If you think, "Wow, if I saw things this way, I would say no, too," you're headed in the right direction.

When you do this analysis, don't just use your imagination to complete the lists. Talk to people who know your counterpart and her company. Do research on what's happening within the company.

Alfredo started in on his lists. Considering what would happen if Deirdre said yes, he realized that she'd have to relocate people, fire others, take the time to hire new employees where perhaps the required specialized skills were in short supply, and explain her decision to the local union with which her company had strong relations. If she said no, Alfredo listed, she'd look strong to her colleagues and her team, keep her promise of no relocations, remain close to her company's headquarters where she could position herself for her next job, continue to have a team of engineers travel to Alfredo's company once a month, and use videoconference the other three weeks. And if things changed for some reason, she could always say yes tomorrow to what would likely be a sweeter deal from Alfredo.

It was no wonder that Deirdre was not saying yes, Alfredo realized; not only did the option on the table go against some of her key interests, but her best alternative was actually sounding pretty good.

Armed with a better understanding of Deirdre's unmet interests, Alfredo could now consider other options; research standards that could help Deirdre defend her choice to others if she did agree to his proposal; or demonstrate that her best alternative was weaker than she thought (perhaps the option to move her department wouldn't last forever!).

4. **Share and check your analysis.** Show your counterpart that you've thought through her perspective and make sure you're on the right track by sharing your conclusions. Say something like, "I was having trouble understanding your point of view, so I tried to list out the reasons you were saying no. What do I have wrong? What am I missing?" Your counterpart will appreciate that you took the time to think through her choice from her perspective, and even if you did a poor job, she'll pick up a pen and begin marking up

your list. This conversation clarifies unmet interests and helps you to move the negotiation back
to inventing new options.

5. **Develop a new proposal.** Try to influence your
counterpart by coming up with a different choice.
This might involve developing a new solution
altogether or simply refining or adding to the one
already on the table. The goal is to find a way to
meet more key interests of hers (as well as meeting your own) and make her alternatives look
weaker, so she'll be more likely to say yes.

Using his analysis, Alfredo created new options that
he felt would be more attractive to Deirdre:

1. Actively assist with recruiting in the new
location.

2. Share criteria on the lower cost of living and
help draft a press release that will address the
concerns of Deirdre's strongest critic—the union.
These standards could help her sell the idea to
her stakeholders.

3. House Deirdre's people for the next six months,
but don't ask them to move permanently.

Notice that the first two options are just slight adjustments to the option that had been on the table all along,
while the third is a very different proposal.

Lastly, Alfredo let Deirdre know that this window of
opportunity wouldn't last forever because the funding for

the move wouldn't be available after the end of the fiscal year. He helped her see that her best alternative—saying no and waiting for him to make a better offer—wasn't as appealing as she thought.

The goal here is to create a new, more appealing option by better understanding the other party's interests. Remember, most people start with a position and hold on to it tightly. Once you understand the reasons behind their grip, you can address their needs and yours with a yesable proposition.

Making understanding a collaborative effort and creating a proposition to which your counterpart can say yes will both help address communication breakdowns and move you toward a more productive solution.

Chapter 13
When Emotions Get in the Way

Go from boiling to cool.

The Problem

Many people fear that no matter how they prepare, their negotiation will spiral into an unproductive debate or a shouting match. Even if you're approaching the negotiation with a collaborative, joint problem-solving mindset, it's possible that things will get heated. You know when it's happening: Perhaps you feel yourself getting emotional; you sense that your blood pressure is rising, that you're becoming angry or anxious. Maybe your counterpart is doing the same. The volume might be getting louder, or perhaps one or both of you have started to yell.

Let's look at an example inside a company doing its annual budget planning. Betty, the head of sales, is preparing her budget for next year, and she's meeting with

Amit, the director of finance. Betty has asked Amit several times for revised numbers that she can include in her budget. Instead of delivering, however, he keeps coming back to her with more questions.

Betty's draft budget is due to the CFO first thing tomorrow morning, so she sends Amit a meeting request to discuss what's going on. Amit accepts, but shows up 15 minutes late. After explaining why she needs the numbers today, Betty asks what's preventing Amit from just giving her the numbers she's asked for. He begins to explain that she hasn't shared enough information and that he's been working hard to make sense of what she *has* given him.

Betty raises her voice: "I've asked you four times to give me those numbers, you showed up late to this meeting, and this is somehow my fault. Why can't you just do what I asked?"

Amit can't believe she's not getting it. "I've been working on your numbers for weeks! But I can't get you the final figures until you give me all the information I need. Don't you understand that this is on you?"

This may not strike you as a negotiation at first glance, but it is: There are two parties, with different incentives and interests, who are trying to come to an agreement about how to proceed. In this case, a conflict has erupted, but it doesn't have to hurt Betty and Amit's relationship or Betty's draft budget.

Why It Happens

Emotions get heated during a negotiation because there are high stakes: people's jobs, their standing with their bosses, their confidence, the success of a venture, or the future of their business.

A negotiation can also get emotional when you and your counterpart haven't communicated well (as we saw in the previous chapter). Perhaps you misunderstood each other's intentions or offended each other by accident, and feelings were hurt.

What to Do About It

Whatever the reason the conversation has turned combative, help your counterpart—or yourself—go from boiling to cool. Remain calm, work to understand what's triggered both of you, see if you can use any of your emotions to help you make your case, and address any systemic problems.

Keep calm

If your counterpart is worked up, try to stay calm. This is easier said than done. Here are a few ways to help defuse the situation:

1. **Focus on your physical reaction.** Breathe deeply rather than tensing up and holding your breath. Ground yourself by putting your hands on the table or your feet on the floor. The physical motions you make will influence how your mind reacts. If you start wringing your hands, you're signaling to your mind that there is something to worry about. On the other hand, if you move slowly and deliberately, you send the message to your brain to remain calm.

2. **Listen to what your counterpart is saying.** Let him vent. Some people need to boil over as a kind of release. After yelling or banging the table, they might calm down by themselves. Don't always feel you need to respond to the outburst. If you can, let it go and move on to a more productive way of interacting.

3. **Show you've heard him.** Calmly paraphrase what you heard. Acknowledging the reason that your counterpart got upset can often help turn things around. Sometimes people just want to be heard.

4. **Show some empathy.** If he's mad because of something that doesn't have anything to do with you, acknowledge that it seems like a tough situation. Perhaps even frame the issue as a joint problem on which you two can work together.

5. **Find out more.** If you're the cause for his frustration, dig in and find out what's happening. Borrowing strategies from the previous chapter, try to understand what you did and how the two of you might be seeing things differently.

6. **Take a break.** If you're the one who's getting angry or emotional, consider taking a break. Go for a walk around the building. Ask someone on your team to help you talk it through. Some deep breathing, or even a little meditation, can help you reground yourself.

When Amit snapped back at her, Betty took a deep breath and sat back in her chair, putting both feet on the ground. With her body steady, she was able to begin calming down, but she couldn't help noticing that Amit still had a red face and crossed arms.

Betty's next step was to apologize for her outburst. She didn't stop there, though. She also asked Amit why he was upset. She moved forward to listen and let him go at it.

Amit said that he was under a lot of pressure given that it was budget time. He admitted that Betty wasn't the first person to get angry with him that week. He talked about how he was missing his targets because he did not get enough resources last year. He even shared a situation two months back when he had asked Betty for help and had gotten nothing. She had no idea what he was referring to, but she didn't stop him; instead, she asked what the consequences had been. With all that off his chest—and with Betty's evident openness to hearing from him—Amit calmed down, too. Betty watched, relieved, as Amit's shoulders began to relax and he uncrossed his arms.

Understand the triggers

As you try to move forward, it's helpful to know what's gotten you worked up in the first place. We all have pet peeves or behaviors that push our buttons. Develop an awareness of what typically makes you upset. Perhaps you don't like it when someone challenges your truthfulness or integrity. Maybe you get mad when someone exaggerates her point or keeps repeating it. Perhaps it's when someone calls you on something you know you need to work on or something you pride yourself on that the person is now framing as a negative. Sometimes simply understanding the underlying reason for your anger can help you regain control.

Pay attention to what makes your counterpart upset as well. Observe when she gets emotional. Are there certain words or behaviors that seem to provoke her? If you've negotiated with her in the past, try to think back to other occasions when she has gotten upset. Do you notice any patterns?

Once Betty and Amit began to calm down, Betty reminded herself that she always got angry when people showed up late to meetings because it made her feel disrespected. She worked many hours in the evening and on the weekends to ensure she was never late, and here not only was Amit late for the meeting, but he was on the verge of making her late submitting her budget. She recognized that this was *her* trigger and that was probably what made her particularly upset.

Betty also remembered that the sales team was known for being overly punctual, and finance just the opposite (perhaps, she now realized, due to the workload created by the demanding sales team). She had worked with Amit for several years and had seen him get upset before: It happened most often when people questioned his work ethic. Amit, too, worked long days, often staying into the evening, and he prided himself on the quality of his work, even if it didn't always get finished on time. To him, working hard and getting things right were more important than meeting a deadline.

Betty suggested that she stay late with Amit that evening so that they could work on the numbers together. Amit would get the information he needed to get the calculations right, and Betty would be able to submit her budget on time. Amit agreed, and both left the meeting feeling much better about the plan and each other.

Use your emotions

Some people think that they aren't supposed to be emotional in a negotiation, that they shouldn't reveal what they're feeling, whether it's good *or* bad. But there are times that showing passion can be helpful. While perhaps Betty derailed the conversation by losing her cool in the meeting, at least Amit now understood how much she cared about getting those numbers and delivering her draft budget on time.

If something upsets you, or if someone pushes your buttons, it's fine to show that you're angry, frustrated, or disappointed. (Reacting without forethought by banging the table, jumping up and down, storming out of the room, or verbally attacking your counterpart, however, is a different story; being out of control is never helpful.) If you're really excited about something positive, such as a feature of the agreement, or something of concern, such as the need to solve a key problem, it's OK to express your passion. Of course, do so as a conscious choice. You certainly don't want to accidentally signal that you're particularly needy (that you care about this interest over all else) or desperate (that your alternatives aren't very good). Instead of letting your emotion control you, harness that emotion and use it to make your point.

You can also harness your counterpart's emotion. Use it to uncover his interests (especially fears or concerns) or as a catalyst to invent options. "You're steaming mad, and I am, too, so what can we do about this?" or "You're clearly hurt. What are some ways we might fix this?" If the person is emotional, he is engaged, and this is often the best time to move into the circle of value. As the emotion dissipates, you might move to sit beside him, focus on a common piece of paper or flip chart, and begin recording interests, options, and standards together.

Address recurring conflicts

Sometimes emotions run high not because of something specific that's happening in the room but because there is a long-standing unhealthy relationship between the two parties. If you sense the underlying reason for your counterpart yelling at you has little to do with what you've just said, try talking about that.

If you're surprised by the negotiation turning emotional, or if negotiations with a particular counterpart turn sour on a consistent basis, it is likely a sign that something systemic is going on. Discover what the underlying cause is: missed deadlines, other broken commitments, lack of preparation, disrespectful comments or behaviors, past threats or escalations, or truth stretched. Use what you learned in chapter 6 about managing the relationship: Explicitly bring these issues up instead of letting them fester, and discuss how to solve the underlying problem rather than just temporarily smoothing things over.

Emotional outbursts can be scary, and it's often hard to imagine how to get past them in the moment. But balancing your and your counterpart's reactions—allowing emotions to be expressed but also thinking analytically about what's really going on and how to address it—helps the conversation stay productive and helps you find solutions that work for everyone.

Section 4
Postgame

Careful review drives learning
and improvement.

How you conclude your negotiation is just as important
as how you begin it. End on the right note so that what
comes next—implementation of the agreement and any
future negotiations—goes smoothly.

In the next chapter, I'll discuss how to wrap up the
negotiation and communicate the results with the right
people. In the final chapter, I'll explain how to learn from
your negotiation to continuously improve your organization's approach to similar transactions, as well as to refine your own skills.

Chapter 14
Wrap Up the Negotiation

Know when you're done, and communicate the final decisions.

If you've successfully negotiated an agreement that meets the criteria you set out earlier for a good outcome, congratulations! It's tough work to get to this point.

You might assume that you've now reached the end of the negotiation and all that's left is the signing of the papers. However, you'll need to take three last steps before considering the negotiation final: documenting the terms, communicating with stakeholders, and prepping for implementation of the agreement.

Document the Terms

If you used the one-text procedure described in the "Get People on the Same Page—Literally" part of chapter 10, you've already written out the terms that you've agreed to. But if you haven't, now is a good time to record where you ended up so that you both have a shared understanding of the specifics.

Incorporate any notes you and your counterpart made along the way, any points you recorded on flip charts or in postsession memos. In a more formal setting, this is where you would create a formal contract that captures your agreement and requires signatures. Whether you use an e-mail, memo, or contract, have your counterpart review and agree to the text, and be sure you each have a copy. Even for quick negotiations in a hallway, you'll likely want to follow up with some sort of written confirmation of your discussion to share with your counterpart and any other stakeholders.

Documenting serves two purposes: One, it ensures that everyone is on the same page. You and your counterpart can share the e-mail or contract as a draft with others in your organizations. Two, the final approved version serves as a record of what you agreed to in case you, your counterpart, or anyone implementing the agreement later needs a reminder of the details.

Caution: Unless you are the sole stakeholder in your party, make clear to your counterpart that you are not yet making a final commitment at this stage. You still need to take your documentation back to your colleagues for review.

Communicate to Make Sure You Have Agreement

Throughout the negotiation, you've been keeping your stakeholders informed. Now is the time to confirm that everyone with decision rights is onboard. Your legal or finance teams may need to review the terms closely, your operations team may be interested in what's coming their way, or perhaps your boss just needs to give her blessing. Share your documentation and explain why you recommend it, focusing on the interests and standards it meets.

Sometimes this review will just be a formality; in other cases, you may need to work to persuade others or, on rare occasion, to revisit parts of the agreement if they have issues.

Whether it's your boss, key functional leaders, or your family, getting those who truly matter onboard will significantly increase your chances of successfully implementing your agreement.

Think Through the Implementation

Before you declare victory and move on, think about what steps will ensure a smooth transition from agreement to implementation.

Perhaps the agreement is something you'll be carrying out yourself, like a new role you just negotiated with your boss. If that's the case, talk about follow-up steps before leaving the room. Who will write up a new job description? Will you need certain resources, and if so, who will acquire them and how? What's the timeline? How will progress be tracked and success be measured? Explicitly discuss how to move from conceptual agreement to action.

If you're wrapping up a more complex negotiation, you'll probably already have addressed important milestones and deadlines and captured them in the con-tract. But before everything is finalized, think one last time about how the agreement will be carried out and by whom, and what could change or go wrong. Have you discussed what happens if you or your counterpart can-not hit these milestones? What process will you use to make adjustments? Will there be any penalties? What happens if you or your counterpart, or other prominent stakeholders, leave your organization before the project is complete? Perhaps you and the other party agreed that there were some risky terms in the agreement and you need to put something up for collateral; if so, what is the plan for doing this?

If your job is simply to negotiate, and you'll hand off the implementation responsibility to others, think about what *they* need to effectively carry out the agreement. These may feel like logistical issues that are extraneous to the negotiation, but in fact they are integral details that you need to consider, discuss with your counterpart, and perhaps also formally add into your documentation. All the work you did to negotiate your agreement will be for naught if it cannot be implemented.

Put the Agreement into Action

Once the agreement is (finally!) final, brief anyone in-volved in its implementation on what has been negoti-ated, the intent behind it, what you've learned about your counterpart and his interests, and any predictable future risks or stumbling blocks. Sharing sticking points from the negotiation process can be helpful as well, since this can indicate where future problems may occur. Certainly take time to explain any element of the agreement that is new to your organization, such as a particularly creative delivery or payment method.

Take, for example, a salesperson for a service provider who just closed a deal. Because of the deal's complexity, the contract required a lot of legal language, so the salesperson should convey the key terms to the delivery team in plain English. The customer emphasized throughout the negotiations concerns about certain deadlines or dependencies, so he should convey those to his delivery team as well. He also noticed during the process that representatives of the customer's organization approached conflict head-on: He'll tell her team that as well, in case disagreements come up over time.

Don't consider the negotiation "finished" until you've conveyed all relevant information about the agreement to anyone who will be working to put it into action; use the "Communicating to Implementers Checklist" box to make sure you've covered everything. Of course, some of these items will not be appropriate in every negotiation. In each case, consider how complex the contract is, how challenging you expect the implementation will be, the depth and dynamics of the past history with this counterpart, and how contentious the negotiation was, and share that with anyone who may be affected by the agreement.

COMMUNICATING TO IMPLEMENTERS CHECKLIST

(1) To help the implementers truly understand the agreement, I have:

- Shared the contract

- Highlighted key points

- Documented our and the other party's core interests behind important terms

- Shared the intent behind terms where it might not be clear

(2) To forewarn them about potential future conflicts, I have:

- Noted where, and why, there was significant contention during the negotiation around a particular issue or term

- Pointed out key areas where there was uncertainty in the negotiation about how to deal with a core issue or difference between the parties

- Highlighted areas where the issue or term creates, leaves open, or tries to manage some substantial risk for either or both parties

- Documented any areas where we are worried about the other party living up to their commitments and any areas where they seem worried about us living up to our commitments

COMMUNICATING TO IMPLEMENTERS CHECKLIST

(3) To assist implementers in managing the ongoing relationship with the other party, I have:

- Shared what I learned from the negotiation about how the other party's organization operates

- Highlighted key differences between our and their priorities, methods, ways of interacting, values, and so on

- Informed them about any relationship tensions, difficult people in the other organization, great people with whom to work, particularly strong and helpful relationships between certain people in our organization and certain people in the other organization, and so on

- Passed on any insights into who influences whom in the other organization, about what kinds of issues, and in what ways: in other words, the details of a fleshed-out Relationship Map for the other organization

(4) To help the implementers get started, I have:

- Made introductions between them and key people in the other party's organization

- Highlighted near-term goals, activities to launch, commitments to be fulfilled, deadlines, and so on

COMMUNICATING TO IMPLEMENTERS CHECKLIST

- Noted any key dependencies between what they need to do and what we need to do, and especially between what we and they committed to do

- Shared how both we and they will be measuring near-term success

Chapter 15
Review What Happened

Use "lessons learned" today for improvement tomorrow.

When the negotiation is truly finished, don't just pat yourself on the back. Every negotiation is an opportunity to learn and to improve your skills as a negotiator.

Set Up a Review

Unfortunately, most people don't formally look back over their negotiations unless things went horribly wrong. Of course, you'll learn a lot from your failures, but there are valuable takeaways from successes, too. Make sure to review, capture what you learned, and get feedback.

Set aside time as close to the end of the negotiation as possible so that the events of the negotiation are still fresh in your mind. For a simpler negotiation, take 15 minutes in your car to think through your lessons learned. For one that's more complex, set up reviews after each session. Consider doing another review after you've lived with the agreement for a few months to gauge if there are things that have come up in the implementation that might cause you to think differently about what to do or avoid the next time you negotiate.

If you negotiated on your own, get help from a trusted colleague and walk her through the process. For a more complex negotiation, set up a meeting with any colleagues who were involved. This includes anyone who was in the room, as well as those who played an important role behind the scenes.

Determine what worked well and where to improve

Identify areas to improve your and your organization's negotiation skills and strategies you may want to use again in other situations.

When you convene this review meeting (or when you sit down to think it through on your own), ask the following questions:

- What worked well? Why? What should I continue doing next time?

- What didn't work well? Why? What should I do differently next time?

- Where did I get stuck in the negotiation and why? If I was able to work my way out, how did I do it?

- Were there things the other party, or his organization, did from which I might learn?

- Are there new interests, creative options, persuasive standards, or effective game-changing moves that I might want to capture to use again or share with colleagues who have similar kinds of negotiations?

For more complex negotiations, consider asking these questions for each phase of the negotiation: preparing, conducting, making midcourse corrections, and closing it out.

Also go back and gauge your final agreement against each of the seven elements as a measure of success. If the agreement meets your interests well, but you can't quite say the same about standards, you now know where you need to prepare or practice more in the future.

Capture what you learned

Document everything discussed in your review session. Be prescriptive. Translate what you've learned into advice to use the next time you negotiate.

Consider keeping a journal that captures lessons from each of your negotiations, including inventive options, compelling standards, ways of improving relationships, or other strategies that worked well for you. That way, you can review these practical tips before your next negotiation and put them to use for a better result.

Share what you've learned with others

Capture your lessons in a way that others who were not part of the process can understand them. Lessons learned in the negotiation too often stay with the negotiator alone. Help others benefit from your experience by highlighting what you learned about the process and the other parties, creative ways you structured the agreement, and successful strategies. Some organizations create negotiation strategy playbooks in which they document this kind of information.

Aim for Continuous Improvement

The best way to get better at negotiation is to prepare, conduct, review, and repeat. While your next negotiation may be about a different set of issues, the process and skills you'll need to be successful are likely quite similar.

If you approach the whole process with discipline, over time you will not only become increasingly confident, you will also achieve better results, build productive relationships, and create valuable agreements with bosses, colleagues, customers, suppliers, and partners alike.

Learn More

If you're interested in learning more about negotiation, the books listed here are a great place to start. These publications are by my colleagues, and each one defined or helped shape the strategies and advice in this guide.

Ertel, Danny, and Mark Gordon. *The Point of the Deal: How to Negotiate When Yes Is Not Enough.* Boston: Harvard Business School Press, 2007.

Fisher, Roger, and Scott Brown. *Getting Together: Building Relationships as We Negotiate.* Boston: Houghton Mifflin, 1988. (Paperback edition: New York: Penguin Books, 1989.)

Fisher, Roger, and Daniel Shapiro. *Beyond Reason: Using Emotions as You Negotiate.* New York: Viking/Penguin, 2005.

Fisher, Roger, William L. Ury, and Bruce Patton. *Getting to YES: Negotiating Agreement Without Giving In,* 2nd edition. New York: Penguin Books, 1991. (1st edition: Boston: Houghton Mifflin, 1981.)

Stone, Douglas, Bruce Patton, and Sheila Heen. *Difficult Conversations: How to Discuss What Matters Most.* New York: Viking/Penguin, 1999.

Index

About the Author

Jeff Weiss is a partner at Vantage Partners, a global consultancy specializing in corporate negotiations, relationship management, partnering, and complex change management. At Vantage, Jeff has led both the Alliances and the Sales Advisory practices, and worked extensively both in the Strategic Sourcing and Supply Chain Management practice and in Vantage's training business. Jeff also serves on the faculties of the Tuck School of Business and the United States Military Academy at West Point, where he is also the codirector of the West Point Negotiation Project.

Notes

Notes

Notes

Notes

Notes

Notes

Notes

Notes

Notes

Notes